THE EFFECTIVE DIRECTOR

Institute of Directors

The IoD supports, represents and sets standards for directors. It is a non party-political business organisation founded by Royal Charter in 1903, currently with around 52,000 members. Membership includes leaders from the complete spectrum of business – from media to manufacturing, e-business to the public sector. Members include CEOs of large corporations as well as entrepreneurial directors of start-up companies. They are represented in 84 per cent of FTSE 100 boards, but 70 per cent are directors of small and medium-sized enterprises.

The IoD offers a wide range of business services including business centre facilities across the UK and on the Continent, conferences, networking events, publications and information services. It provides authoritative representation of the interests of business to UK government and EU policymakers, enabling business leaders' views to be influential in the development of public policy.

In response to the increasingly global nature of business, the IoD has founded IoD International, delivering training overseas, and the IoD International Network, its worldwide branches and affiliates. The network promotes excellence in corporate governance and aims to have a significant impact on the international business environment.

A key objective of the IoD is to promote professionalism in the boardroom. It has established a highly regarded qualification for directors – Chartered Director – and runs specific board and director-level training and individual career mentoring programmes.

Director Publications supports the professional activities of the institute through a number of core publications. These include *The Director's Handbook* (2007) and *The Effective Director* (2008), which follows on from *Standards for the Board* (2006).

For more information call +44 (0)20 7766 8888 or visit www.iod.com

AN INSTITUTE OF DIRECTORS
PUBLICATION

THE EFFECTIVE DIRECTOR

building individual and board success

Neville Bain

First published in Great Britain by Director Publications Ltd for the Institute of Directors, 116 Pall Mall, London SW1Y 5ED.

Distributed by Kogan Page Ltd, 120 Pentonville Road, London N1 9JN.

A CIP record for this book is available from the British Library.

ISBN: 978 0749450267

Designed by Halo Design, London. Printed and bound in Great Britain by The Westdale Press Ltd.

about this book

Director development has been, and continues to be, a key activity of the Institute of Directors. The institute helps raise standards not only through programmes such as Chartered Director, its professional qualification for directors, and seminars and courses, but also through specialist publications.

The Director's Handbook, first published in 2005 and recently updated in light of the Companies Act 2006, sets out the legal duties, responsibilities and liabilities of directors. This book complements it. A guide to best boardroom practice, it is based not just on statutory and voluntary codes of conduct, on good theory, but also on close observation of effective directors. It is a core publication for the IoD and references *Standards for the Board*, last published by the IoD in 2006.

The Effective Director is broad in scope and includes dedicated chapters on small and medium-sized companies, and charities and not-for-profit organisations (NPOs). It is written for anyone who wants to improve the effectiveness of their organisation, be it an NPO, a family company, a private business or a member of the FTSE 100.

It will assist all Company Direction programme delegates and will be particularly helpful to those pursuing the Diploma and Chartered Director, but is not aimed at them exclusively. It is for anyone committed to the principle of continuous professional development – whether or not they're IoD members, whether they're new or experienced members of the board.

The Effective Director covers the standards of governance required of listed companies and will therefore relate directly to directors considering floating their businesses. However, since these standards are accepted by a wide variety of organisations, they have virtually universal relevance.

Much of the content applies internationally, and it is expected that this will be reflected in the readership.

The book is neither prescriptive nor dogmatic. My approach is to share my experiences and draw on the bank of research undertaken by the institute. The book is an *insight* into the workings of a more effective board and the real benefit of a structure of good governance. It includes a number of case studies that supplement key points and are based on real companies and real events.

No mystery surrounds those who succeed as directors in organisations. They are well informed and know the legal framework in which they operate. They ensure that the right people are appointed to the right roles, that they are motivated to succeed and that they are developed for the future; they understand that talent is a precious resource that must not be wasted. They want employees to be a credit to the organisation – but, just as importantly, they want the organisation to be a credit to employees.

They understand the need for appropriate processes – processes that are light of touch but add real value.

They have an ethical map that guides them and those in the organisation to make great decisions that are consistent with organisational values.

Strategic evaluation and implementation, and risk assessment and control, are essential components in their effectiveness.

People who serve on boards, or aspire to do so, want to add value to their organisations and make a lasting contribution. Like those they employ, they want job satisfaction. *The Effective Director* will help them fulfil their aims. Readers will be able to dip in and out of the book, gathering both the general and specific information they need.

The book begins with a series of core or general chapters, covering the role of the board, the duties and liabilities of directors, governance and the key board committees. Subsequent chapters cover the softer, but equally vital, area of building effectiveness and value through leadership and people. The last section discusses the special topics of small and medium-sized companies, so important in economies around the world, and charities and the not-for-profit sector. It concludes with a discussion on ethics and values.

The final chapter summarises the book's key messages. It should provide the impetus for a review of personal performance and alert the reader to the key governance challenges they face.

Neville Bain
London, September 2007

"The demands on directors have never been higher. The competition is tougher; the pressures from shareholders ever greater; and the regulatory environment ever more complex. Today's director has not just to deliver results but to do so under intense scrutiny. This book should prove an invaluable guide to the key features of the role."

Sir George Cox, chairman of the Design Council and board member of NYSE-Euronext

"This book would be valuable for all directors – whether of public or private companies or those filling equivalent roles in not-for-profit organisations. It should be especially helpful to all those who are seeking to improve performance or who are seeking to take on the role in new organisations. I especially applaud the emphasis on nurturing and growing talent to improve organisational and personal effectiveness."

Richard Boggis-Rolfe, chief executive of UK and international executive search company, Odgers Ray and Berndtson

"This easy reference guide will help entrepreneurs match individual flair to best practice in the boardroom."

John Timpson, chairman of privately owned shoe-repair and key-cutting company, Timpson

"In a period of great turmoil in the global corporation, this book brings a breath of fresh air and sound reasoning to the critical role of corporate governance."

Professor Charles Cooney, innovation faculty director at Massachusetts Institute of Technology (MIT) and board member of global biotechnology corporation, Genzyme

"I found Neville Bain's book very useful. It helped me become a more effective non-executive director of the two Indian-based companies on whose boards I serve."

Professor Catherine Rosenberg, University Research Chair at the University of Waterloo, Canada

"This is an excellent work of international importance. We will use this book in Russia as a valuable set piece for our directors."

Alexander Ikonnikov, chairman of the Independent Directors Association (IDA), which aims to raise corporate governance standards in Russia, and a non-executive director of Baltika, Russia's largest brewer; Alexander Filatov, CEO of the IDA and an independent director of Russia's Second Power-Generating Company

about the author

Neville Bain, current chairman of the Institute of Directors, was born and educated in New Zealand. He has a double bachelor degree in accounting and economics, a master of commerce with honours and has been awarded a doctor of laws by Otago University. He is a fellow of the IoD and a fellow of the Royal Society of Medicine.

He started his career as a chartered accountant in New Zealand and then spent 27 years with Cadbury Schweppes, working first as finance and export director in NZ, then moving to general management in South Africa. In 1980, he was appointed to the main board in London as group strategy director and went on to run the worldwide confectionery business. His last appointment with Cadbury Schweppes was as deputy group chief executive and finance director.

In 1990, he was headhunted to become the chief executive of the textile, clothing and fashion business, Coats Viyella.

Since 1996, he has held a number of non-executive roles with high-profile British businesses and invested in and acted as an adviser to small and medium-sized companies. He has been chairman of the Royal Mail (1997 to 2001), SHL Group (1998 to 2003) and Hogg Robinson (1997 to July 2006). From 1997 until May 2007, he was a non-executive director of Scottish & Newcastle, where he also chaired the audit committee.

He currently sits on the boards of Biocon, the Indian biotechnology company, and Provexis, a UK functional food company, and chairs two pension trustee boards.

Dr Bain has published papers on the effective management of people, governance, the audit committee and risk assessment and control.

He has also written three previous books, all published by Macmillan: *Successful Management*, 1995; *Winning Ways through Corporate Governance*, 1996 with David Band; and *The People Advantage*, 2000 with Bill Mabey.

He became chairman of the IoD in May 2006.

contents

list of figures and case studies

helping the board do better

All organisations want to succeed. Companies want long-term profitability and growth for the benefit of shareholders and stakeholders. Public sector bodies strive to be effective and efficient with taxpayers' money. Charities need to secure the resources to continue their work – and to do it well. An organisation is an often complex network of people, scattered across departments and locations, but it is ultimately only as good as those who lead it. It is those on the board who decide the strategy and goals, manage the risks, set the tone and create the culture. This makes the question "How can the board do better?" imperative.

This book is written for all practising directors, and explains how the collective and individual performance of members of the board can be improved and what being an effective director actually means. Drawn from the extensive personal experience of the author, it is based on proven best practice. It shows how directors (and their equivalents) can add real value to their organisations and, in the process, gain a strong sense of satisfaction from their roles.

Miles Templeman
Director General, Institute of Directors

improving professional standards

As a Chartered Director, and the chairman of the IoD's Professional Accreditation Committee (PAC), I welcome and commend this book. The PAC's main objectives are to raise the professional standards of directors and persuade organisations and individuals (across all sectors) that properly functioning and balanced boards are the key to added value.

Directorship brings with it significant responsibilities. It requires special attributes and abilities, and understanding of legal duties and statutory and regulatory codes. And it requires a willingness to learn and to change.

Directors have a duty to update their knowledge and skills; to be equipped for the challenge of today and tomorrow.

The Effective Director provides a core text that highlights what individuals need to do to be better informed, to fulfil their duties more effectively and to improve their performance to deliver greater success. This book is also an excellent grounding for the Company Direction programme, which leads to the Chartered Director qualification. It strongly supports continuing professional development.

Peter Hammonds
Chairman, Professional Accreditation Committee, Institute of Directors

acknowledgements

In writing this book, I've drawn upon the experience and expertise of the directors and staff of the Institute of Directors. They have provided material, suggestions and helpful comments as this work has progressed. However, responsibility for the work remains mine alone. The personal views expressed throughout this text are also my responsibility and may not always reflect the views of the institute.

It is always dangerous to single out individuals, but I feel that I especially need to recognise the contributions of the people below.

Tom Nash, publishing director at the IoD, is a significant supporter of this book. Tom was responsible for suggesting that I undertake this work and has provided the encouragement needed to finish the job.

Contributions were made by Peter Hammonds and other members of the institute's Professional Accreditation Committee and by Janet Gardner, head of professional standards at the IoD. Ingrid Farmer and Patricia Peter of the IoD also provided assistance with research and made valuable suggestions, especially in the important area of governance.

I also wish to acknowledge four of my IoD board colleagues.

Sir Hugh Sykes kindly provided the material for the case study of Mid Yorkshire Hospitals Trust, included in chapter 10.

Ian Dormer provided a number of helpful observations for chapter 9 on small and medium-sized companies.

Philippa Foster Back provided material from the Institute of Business Ethics, which helped me with chapter 11, and additionally provided advice and insights for this chapter.

Peter Holland provided helpful legal input in a number of areas.

I was privileged to have the very talented Caroline Proud sub-editing this book. She has challenged, corrected and improved the original text, for which I am extremely grateful.

Finally, my thanks also to Gary Parfitt of Halo Design for the clarity of the page layout and the stylish design of the cover.

Neville Bain

the role of the board

CHAPTER 1

Introduction

A company is a separate legal entity from those who manage it and those who have put up the capital. The key parties are the shareholders, the creditors and the directors. The directors must act in the best interests of the company at all times and not represent any special group of shareholders.

Increasingly, companies recognise that their success depends on those employed in the business and on being "good citizens" in the communities in which they operate. Boards are aware that stakeholders' interests need to be reflected in decision-making if they are to act in the best interests of the company.

Stakeholders typically include creditors, employees, customers, suppliers and communities. Consequently, responsible operating will include making concern for people and the environment a key part of policy and practice. Many companies will, for example, report annually on their compliance with environmental policy, often retaining an objective third party for this purpose.

At the same time, the directors are looking to add long-term value through the execution of a well thought-through strategy in a competitive and changing world.

Are we getting the most from our boards?

Many corporations are failing to obtain full value from their boards, say Chris Thomas, David Kidd and Claudio Fernandez-Araoz in the 2007 winter issue of the *MIT Sloan Management Review*. This lost opportunity not only applies to dysfunctional boards but also to successful companies. The authors say their research highlights five key problems.

☐ **Inadequate competencies.** While most directors are capable, they lack the competence to deal with difficult, sensitive issues. Only 60 per cent of the directors in the research sample believe that all board members understand the key operating issues or the main sources of risk. (This is borne out by own experience, and is a compelling argument for making risk assessment and control a key issue for directors.)

The MIT Sloan research also finds that 70 per cent of directors believe that their colleagues are inadequately prepared for meetings, and just 60 per cent feel all directors participate effectively.

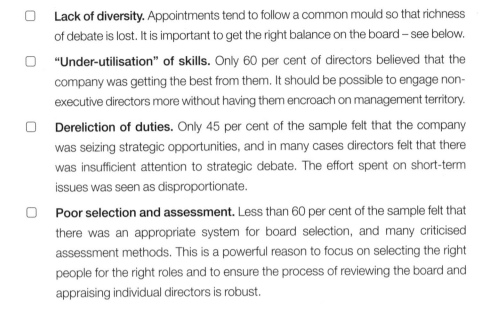

- ☐ **Lack of diversity.** Appointments tend to follow a common mould so that richness of debate is lost. It is important to get the right balance on the board – see below.

- ☐ **"Under-utilisation" of skills.** Only 60 per cent of directors believed that the company was getting the best from them. It should be possible to engage non-executive directors more without having them encroach on management territory.

- ☐ **Dereliction of duties.** Only 45 per cent of the sample felt that the company was seizing strategic opportunities, and in many cases directors felt that there was insufficient attention to strategic debate. The effort spent on short-term issues was seen as disproportionate.

- ☐ **Poor selection and assessment.** Less than 60 per cent of the sample felt that there was an appropriate system for board selection, and many criticised assessment methods. This is a powerful reason to focus on selecting the right people for the right roles and to ensure the process of reviewing the board and appraising individual directors is robust.

Board composition

The company's articles of association will prescribe the way directors are to be appointed, and often a minimum and maximum number of directors. For companies with a full listing on the London Stock Exchange, there will be further requirements under the Combined Code on Corporate Governance. (Note that the Code does not apply to AIM-listed companies and includes some concessions for smaller companies; see chapter 9 for information specific to SMEs.)

Key to a successful, productive board is a good balance. There should be a mix of independent non-executive directors and executive directors and, importantly, of skills and experience.

The Combined Code says that at least 50 per cent of the members of the board should be independent directors and that the roles of chairman and chief executive should be separated. Further, it says that the chairman should not be a former chief executive. When companies believe they have good reason to go against these recommendations, they need to state their case in their annual reports. (The Code's regime is one of comply or explain – see Appendix I.)

The board will work best if non-executives have a variety of experiences, skills and backgrounds: diversity will add the most value to debate and decisions.

Non-executive directors are appointed through the nomination committee after a rigorous process that starts with a definition of the role and a description of the competencies and experience sought. The nomination committee makes its recommendations to the members of the board, who make the final decision on appointments.

Typically, board composition and effectiveness are examined by the chairman annually. A longer term view of the board is taken as part of the succession planning process.

In Figure 1.1 there is an action list for deciding who sits on the board.

FIGURE 1.1
ACTION LIST FOR DECIDING BOARD COMPOSITION

☐ Consider the ratio of non-executive to executive directors

☐ Think of the future needs of the business; consider the energy, experience, knowledge, skills and personal attributes of current and prospective directors; ensure there's a proper process for appointing directors

☐ Consider the cohesion of the board and the chemistry between the directors when making new appointments

☐ Make succession plans for members of the board and senior executives and update them regularly

☐ Agree the procedures for appointing the chairman and the chief executive

☐ Appoint a nomination committee whose terms of reference ensure that: the range of potential candidates is wide; recommendations are made to the board only after a rigorous selection process

☐ Assess the contribution of each director in an annual review. (The chairman should lead the review and arrange individual development programmes where necessary or, in cases of persistent unsatisfactory performance, ask the director to leave the company.)

☐ Provide new members with a comprehensive induction programme

---

Four key tasks of the board

In the IoD publication, *Standards for the Board*, four key tasks of the board are identified. These can be accessed at www.iod.com/chartered.

The four key tasks can be summarised as:

☐   establish and maintain vision, mission and values;

☐   decide the strategy and the structure;

☐   delegate authority to management and monitor and evaluate the implementation of policies, strategies and business plans;

☐   account to shareholders and be responsible to stakeholders.

The terms of the first task need defining.

☐   **Vision** is a view of the future state of the company. The best visions give a picture of the potential of the company and therefore inspire people; a leader uses a "vision" to describe to colleagues what the company can be and to urge them to achieve.

☐   **Mission** is a statement of what needs to be done in order to achieve the envisaged state.

☐   **Values** are a set of principles, standards of conduct and deeply held beliefs; a leadership style that drives the decision-making of the company.

All four tasks are explained further in the appendix to this chapter. It's important to remember that to carry them out effectively, the boardroom processes have to be right. Directors need clear terms of reference and good reporting channels.

Matters reserved to the board

One of the board's earliest jobs is to decide the way it will work and to identify and agree the things that cannot be delegated. Following on from that, and cascading through the organisation, will be a delegation of powers – to the executive committee, the subsidiary boards where applicable, and the senior management.

Matters reserved to the board should be reviewed annually to ensure currency and relevance. They will include not only those powers that no board should surrender, but also items that relate to the particular needs of the organisation.

Set out below in Figure 1.2 is an example of a statement of reserved matters in a fairly generic form. This is followed in Figure 1.3 by a list of items reserved to the board of the Institute of Directors.

Figure 1.3 also refers to delegated powers.

FIGURE 1.2
EXAMPLE OF STATEMENT OF RESERVED MATTERS

1. Statutory obligations

1.1 Approval of:

- [ ] the interim report and dividend;
- [ ] the annual report and accounts;
- [ ] the final dividend;
- [ ] circulars to shareholders, including those convening meetings.

1.2 Consideration of returns to overseas stock exchanges where applicable

1.3 Recommending to shareholders:

- [ ] changes to the Memorandum and Articles of Association;
- [ ] proposals relating to the appointment and removal of auditors and the approval of their fee (although this is often delegated to the audit committee).

2. Strategic and financial matters

2.1 Consideration of:

- [ ] the company vision, mission and values, and any changes to them;
- [ ] the strategy and the annual review of it;
- [ ] budgets, and regular review of progress against them, and the delivery of strategic milestones.

2.2 Approval of:

- [ ] treasury, risk management and capital policies, including funding and the issue of new shares of any class and of loan capital in excess of a prescribed value;
- [ ] capital expenditure in excess of agreed levels, acquisitions, joint ventures and disposals;
- [ ] significant changes in accounting policy. (These would usually be first approved by the audit committee and noted by the board.)

3. Human resource matters

3.1 Approval of:

- [ ] the appointment or removal of the managing director, other executive directors or the company secretary;
- [ ] the appointment or removal of other directors recommended by the nomination committee.

The roles and duties of the chairman and managing director and their discretionary powers.

The arrangement of directors' and officers' liability insurance.

4. Other matters

4.1 Approval of:

- [ ] any matter that would have a material impact on the company's financial position, liabilities, future strategy or reputation;
- [ ] significant contracts not in the ordinary course of the business;
- [ ] health and safety policy. (This should be reviewed across the business to reflect changes such as new risks and new regulations);
- [ ] values statements and systems to monitor how the organisation's values apply in practice.

4.2 Delegation of:

- [ ] the board's powers and authority to sub-committees that will regularly report to the board and make minutes of their meetings available to the board.

Committees of the board

The board delegates powers to its main committees and lays out formal terms and conditions for them, which it reviews annually. The Combined Code on Corporate Governance and the Stock Exchange Listing Rules oblige a company to have three committees of the board – the audit, remuneration and nomination committees. Chapter 5 looks at these committees in detail, particularly the audit committee, which has a pivotal role in governance.

Other committees

Depending on the size and nature of the organisation, other committees may be necessary.

In businesses with significant borrowings in multi-currencies there may be a case for a **treasury committee**. This is chaired by a non-executive and consists of the finance director and a specialist group of non-executive directors who, together, review treasury policy, taking into account the company's exposure to fluctuations in foreign exchange rates and interest rates and its need to protect overseas assets. Where there are banking covenants or agency credit assessments to rate the company debt, the treasury committee will monitor these at quarterly meetings. The committee will recommend to the board changes in policy, having diligently reviewed proposals and alternatives. The board takes a good deal of comfort in the fact that this complex area receives the detailed scrutiny of non-executives with experience in accountancy and finance.

In some companies, there will be a separate **health and safety committee**. Obvious examples include airlines, railways and petrochemical businesses, where health and safety risks and hazards are potentially high. The committee will monitor compliance with health and safety guidelines throughout the business and put right any discovered breaches.

In a number of cases, **risk assessment and control** is taken away from the audit committee, which many observers feel is overloaded, and given to a separate group. My preference is not to do this: audit and risk are too mutually dependent to be dealt with by separate committees.

FIGURE 1.3
INSTITUTE OF DIRECTORS
LEVELS OF AUTHORITY AND AUTHORISATION PROCEDURES

Matters Reserved to the Board

(Please note that the IoD policy is to go beyond statutory obligations and observe best practice principles, as laid down by the Combined Code.)

Companies Act requirements

- ☐ Approval of annual report and accounts
- ☐ Approval of any significant change in accounting policy
- ☐ Appointment or removal of the institute secretary
- ☐ Remuneration of auditors, and recommendations for appointment or removal of auditors

Management

- ☐ Approval of the institute's principal commercial and policy strategies
- ☐ Approval of the institute's annual operating budget
- ☐ Approval of the institute's annual capital expenditure budget
- ☐ Terms and conditions of employment of directors or other staff and their service contracts if the salary exceeds £100k pa or the term of office exceeds six months (except to the extent that such matters are referred by the board to the remuneration committee)
- ☐ Major changes to the institute's management and control structure

Board membership and board committees

- ☐ Board appointments and removals
- ☐ Terms of reference of chairman, deputy chairmen, director general, chief operating officer and other executive directors
- ☐ Terms of reference and membership of board committees

Cadbury recommendations

- ☐ Major capital projects (above £300k in budget or £150k unbudgeted)
- ☐ Major long-term arrangements, e.g. contract or lease where the institute's obligations last for three years or more (unless the total payments/cost to the institute is less than £150k); material contract or lease lasting for one year or more that grants

another party sole rights in relation to the institute or that restricts the institute from carrying on any particular activity

- ☐ Material contracts of the institute or any subsidiary in the course of ordinary business, e.g. loans and repayments above £300k
- ☐ Investments or disposals above £300k
- ☐ Risk management strategy – any material changes
- ☐ Health and safety policy – any material changes
- ☐ Treasury policies and strategy amounting to a significant change

Miscellaneous

- ☐ Trustees or rules of the institute's pension schemes – any significant changes
- ☐ Benefits under any pension scheme or other employee benefit arrangement – any significant changes
- ☐ Prosecution, defence or settlement of litigation involving sums above £250k, or being otherwise material to the interests of the institute
- ☐ Environment policy – any significant changes
- ☐ Ethics policy and social responsibility policy – any significant changes
- ☐ Published policies – significant change in the institute's stance on public (i.e. external) policy issues or the adoption and/or publication of a stance on a significant public issue
- ☐ Donations policy – significant changes (on the understanding that donations to political parties should never be made because of the institute's apolitical platform)
- ☐ Directors' and officers' liability insurance – any material changes
- ☐ Executive directors' external interests and any external interests of non-executive directors that may conflict with the activities of the IoD
- ☐ Common seal and deeds – policy on use of common seal and the execution of deeds
- ☐ Internal control arrangements – any significant change
- ☐ Closure, creation or merger of branch, division or region
- ☐ Procedures for conduct of business and activities of regions and branches – any significant changes
- ☐ Professional qualifications offered by the institute – any significant change in nature

Improving the board's performance

The board is always capable of improving its performance. No board has reached a state of perfection. And states of near-perfection can never be taken for granted. The board constantly needs to fine-tune its performance if it's to be sure of being able to respond quickly and appropriately to changes in the wider environment.

The Combined Code recommends that the effectiveness of the board is reviewed annually, and that the senior non-executive, after discussion with directors, assesses the chairman's performance annually. The wise chairman will, at least once a year, hold one-to-one meetings with the non-executives to discover what they see as his/her strengths and weaknesses and where his/her contribution could be improved.

Some boards ask an independent third party such as the Institute of Directors to carry out the appraisal. This can be a way of maximising objectivity and credibility. However, boards that have the necessary emotional maturity can do the exercise equally well in house. The in-house approach often takes the form of a questionnaire, with the results collated by a trusted person such as the company secretary. Some companies, for example, Scottish & Newcastle, use the questionnaire as the basis for discussion and then have the company secretary and the head of internal audit conduct interviews and compile the report.

Whatever the approach, the performance review, if sufficiently robust, can be an enlightening and value-adding exercise.

Sir Christopher Hogg, former chief executive of Vodafone and non-executive chairman of GlaxoSmithKline, has observed that there are three principal questions to ask when judging a board's effectiveness:

☐   is the entire board fully engaged in and contributing to the strategy?

☐   does the board effectively review its own performance?

☐   does it give sufficient time to succession planning?

Figure 1.4 shows the questionnaire used by the IoD for its latest board evaluation. *Chapter 4 includes a template for a board effectiveness review at a FTSE 100 company – see Figure 4.2.*

Information for the board

Newly appointed directors must have an induction programme that will help them get up to speed as quickly as possible. The precise content of this programme will vary from director to director. However, there are some core elements. Discussions with the key executives are one; the provision of information is another.

The list of information for **new directors** will include:

- [ ] the latest strategy document, showing the key milestones and progress to date;

- [ ] the budget for the current year and the company's progress against it;

- [ ] minutes of the past year's meetings and a list of any significant developments that are being considered in the current year;

- [ ] details of any significant legal actions or major disputes;

- [ ] a review (where relevant) of the latest analysts' notes, including the broker's note.

Thereafter, the director should receive the information they need to monitor the business. This will include regular, up-to-date financial statements and information on everything that materially affects the business or could do so. Many medium and larger companies use a form of "balanced scorecard", so that dimensions beyond finance are included in the regular reports. Scope typically includes the marketplace and customers, human resources, key business processes and, perhaps, the supplier or cost base. The reports will start with a review of the wider environment, including government regulation and competitors, and then move on to the specific areas.

Each director will also, of course, receive minutes of meetings. These should be agreed and circulated quickly – if possible, within seven days.

Many companies give non-executives electronic access to the top level of their databases and allow them to request permission to "interrogate" the lower levels.

Special attention needs to be given to the strategy discussion, which is often reserved for dedicated "away days". Knowledge of macro market trends, competitor analysis and assessment of the success of the current strategy make for a better, more informed debate. While presentations from executives are an important feature of these meetings, sufficient time must be allowed for the input of the non-executives.

FIGURE 1.4
THE INSTITUTE OF DIRECTORS BOARD EFFECTIVENESS REVIEW

A. Leadership

1. Does the board provide sufficient leadership to the institute?
2. Does the board clearly set the institute's strategic aims?
3. Does the board ensure that the necessary financial and human resources are in place for the institute to meet its objectives?
4. Does the board review management performance appropriately?
5. Is there an appropriate management development and succession planning process?
6. Does the board set and support the company's mission, vision, strategic objectives and values?
7. Does the board take the time to ensure that the values are maintained across the institute?
8. Are the processes for discussing and setting strategy, the strategic plan and the annual budget appropriate?

B. Board Composition

1. Is the board of the right size?
2. Does the board have the right balance of: executive and non-executive directors; skills; independent non-executive directors.
3. Is the division of responsibilities between the chairman and director general clear and appropriate?
4. Are there constructive relations between executive and non-executive directors?

C. Board Meetings

1. Does the board meet sufficiently regularly to discharge its duties effectively?
2. Is sufficient time allowed for debate?
3. Is the formal schedule of matters specifically referred for the board's decision appropriate?
4. Does the chairman hold annual meetings with non-executive directors without the executives present?
5. Do the non-executives add value by providing good challenge and judgment but stop short of interfering with the detailed management?
6. Are board and committee papers clear, of the right level of detail and supplied in a timely manner?
7. Do the board minutes properly record discussion and, where appropriate, individual or collective reservations or concerns?
8. Are board dinners and interfaces with senior management effective?
9. Do all board directors make an effective contribution at meetings?
10. Is the quality of debate open and robust?
11. Do board discussions reach satisfactory closure?
12. Does the secretariat provide the right level of service?

D. Appointments to the Board

1. Is the procedure for appointment of new directors to the board sufficiently formal, rigorous and transparent?
2. Are appointments to the board made on merit and against objective criteria?
3. Are plans in place for an orderly succession for appointments to the board and to senior management?
4. Is the membership of the nomination committee appropriate?
5. Are the terms of reference of the nomination committee clear and appropriate?
6. Is committee membership regularly refreshed?

E. Information and Professional Development

1. Is the board supplied in a timely manner with information in a form and of a quality appropriate to enable it to discharge its duties?

2. Do directors receive an appropriate induction on joining the board?

3. Do directors regularly update and refresh their skills and knowledge?

4. Should there be a formal recording of director hours on training and continuous professional development?

5. Is the information flow between the board and its committees and between senior management and non-executive directors of sufficient frequency and quality?

6. Are committees provided with sufficient resources to undertake their duties?

F. Performance Evaluation

1. Is the annual performance evaluation for the board, committees and individual directors sufficiently formal and rigorous?

2. Does the institute act on the results of the performance evaluation appropriately?

G. Remuneration

1. Are levels of remuneration in the institute sufficient to attract, retain and motivate senior management and executive directors without the institute paying more than is necessary for this purpose?

2. Is the remuneration committee sensitive to pay and employment conditions in arenas competing for our senior staff?

3. Does the remuneration committee receive up-to-date advice on developments in remuneration elsewhere?

4. Do the performance-related elements of remuneration form an appropriate proportion of the total remuneration package of executive directors and senior managers?

5. Is the make-up of the remuneration committee appropriate?

6. Are the terms of reference of the remuneration committee clear and appropriate? Is the procedure for developing policy on executive remuneration and for fixing the remuneration packages of

individual directors sufficiently formal and transparent?

H. Internal Control

1. Is the system of internal control sufficiently sound to safeguard institute investments and assets?

2. Are the arrangements for identifying, evaluating, monitoring and mitigating risks appropriate?

3. Are we satisfied that management has embedded risk assessment and control in the decision-making of the institute?

4. Is the make-up of the audit committee appropriate?

5. Does at least one member of the audit committee have recent and relevant financial experience?

6. Are the terms of reference of the audit committee clear and appropriate?

7. Are the arrangements by which institute staff may, in confidence, raise concerns about possible improprieties in financial reporting or other matters appropriate?

8. Where auditors provide non-audit services, are appropriate arrangements in place to ensure that auditor objectivity and independence are safeguarded?

I. Membership

1. Does the institute maintain an appropriate dialogue with its members?

2. Do we communicate effectively with the membership?

3. Is the board seen to be acting in the best interests of members in general?

J. Generally

1. In what areas in your view has the board performed most effectively?

2. In what areas in your view is the board least effective?

3. Is there anything that you feel we need to spend more time addressing?

The preparation and agreement of the budget is a very important item on the agenda and should not be rushed. The assumptions will need to be tested, and the expected results measured against the relevant year of the strategy and, in the case of a listed company, the expectations of the City.

Other periodic exercises that require information to be supplied to the board include:

- [ ] management development and succession plans;
- [ ] health and safety reviews;
- [ ] risk assessment and control, and the identification of the high-level risks;
- [ ] comparison of share price trends with index and peer group (for listed companies);
- [ ] a review of significant shareholdings.

Testing the statement of values

The statement of values is one of the key board statements but it means little without the behaviours that support it.

Assessing the extent to which values are *embedded* in the organisation – in the way it works, the way it is managed – is a vital exercise. But too few boards approach it in a formal or systematic way.

To build and maintain the company's reputation, boards should look once a year at the way the statement of values applies in practice. Directors may get a sense of the importance of values in the decision-making process in the way that projects or proposals are put to the board. It can, for example, be relatively easy to spot the senior manager whose commitment to ethics and corporate social responsibility does not extend beyond complying with the letter of the law. International companies often operate in countries where bribes are routinely needed to secure contracts, and directors will need to be vigilant if they're to ensure that the company's values are applied universally.

Individual directors should spend time talking to key people in their own environments and getting more insights into the values of the company.

Some approaches review the way that customers and suppliers are treated or the way employees are encouraged and rewarded. Surveys of employees, customers and suppliers can help test the statement of values against the reality of what's going on. Such surveys are best carried out by professional third parties.

Appointing a new chief executive

The appointment of a new chief executive is one of the most important decisions a board can face. It is vitally important to get the right leadership to release the talent from the team, and to have the right experience to move the organisation forward. There may well be executives within the organisation that would lay claim to the role, and succession planning may have included the development of those considered contenders. (Much will depend on the extent to which the departure of the current chief executive was planned.) The lead internal candidate will have been identified before the incumbent leaves.

The nomination committee will typically require an external search.

The case for an external appointment is compelling where significant change is needed. At former monopoly Royal Mail, for example, the board judged that only someone from outside the organisation could lead it into the new commercial realities of full competition. Adam Crozier, former head of the advertising agency Saatchi and Saatchi and the Football Association, was brought in.

What are the rules for appointing a chief executive? Good practice suggests the following:

- [ ] understand the strengths and personality styles of the current top team;

- [ ] clarify from the strategy the key drivers of value for the next five years;

- [ ] understand the implications of the two points above for the experience and competencies required for a new chief executive;

- [ ] prepare a job description and a profile of the ideal candidate, clearly identifying the business needs;

- [ ] take stock of the lead internal candidate and establish how closely the fit of skills is to the business needs;

- [ ] brief a search consultant, preferably one that has previous knowledge of the organisation;

- [ ] shortlist external candidates;

- [ ] ask the consultant to interview and evaluate the internal candidate;

- [ ] involve non-executives outside the nomination committee in the selection process – their input can be invaluable.

The nomination committee will receive written reports on candidates (which may include the results of psychometric tests) and will interview the shortlist itself. When a preferred candidate emerges, references should be taken and any concerns followed up before making an offer and agreeing terms.

The potential consequences of mishandling the selection of the new chief executive are set out in the Cosgrove case study below.

CASE STUDY: COSGROVE MANUFACTURING PLC

Cosgrove was a FTSE 350 conglomerate operating in a number of traditional sectors and with a significant traditional manufacturing base in the UK. It produced ingredients for food products, a selection of condiments under a retail brand that was marketed solely in the UK, and also "own label" products for the big retailers. Another division produced enzymes for use in textiles, among other industries, and for bio fuel, and had a specialist engineering company.

The company had grown over 50 years from small beginnings. It owed much to the entrepreneurial zeal of the founder, a strong individual of Turkish origin.

The founder had floated the company 10 years ago to free up some personal capital and to provide equity for an acquisition. He was, until 1997, both chairman and chief executive, with a stake of 25 per cent in his and his family's name.

Increased competition meant that earnings were static, to the displeasure of the City, which was already uncomfortable with the founder's lack of communication and autocratic style.

The board decided that the roles of chairman and chief executive needed to be split. There were three internal candidates for CEO but none was seen to have the skills to lead the group or to bring about change – or to counter the founder, who, as executive chairman, watched every move.

In 1997, two candidates for CEO were put forward by the search agent. The founder insisted on doing several one-to-one interviews with both of them. The candidates were concerned by his style and approach.

The chosen chief executive, Stephen Oakes, came from the branded food industry and agreed to an initial term appointment of three years. During that time, the group was re-structured, skills across the company were raised and new people introduced. The company made financial and strategic progress.

What if things go wrong?

Adherence to legal requirements and knowledge of the principles and provisions of the Combined Code (accepted by a wide variety of organisations as the blueprint for best practice) are essential: they form the framework for good governance. They do not, however, guarantee that things will not go wrong.

In 2000, there was one internal candidate capable of taking over from Oakes, but the chairman did not feel the chemistry was right and he vetoed the appointment. Oakes agreed to stay for up to another year while they sought a chief executive from outside.

The selection process, however, was flawed: the board had become fixated on the need to hire someone capable of working with the chairman. No job specification was prepared, and no thought given to the qualities needed to take the company to the next stage of its development.

There was no nomination committee, and the chairman started to interview people he knew and people suggested by a "friendly" head hunter. After about six months, feeling that change needed to be made soon, the board endorsed Mervyn Frost. Recently made redundant from a FTSE 250 engineering company, Frost was well known to the chairman. He seemed from the start not to engage with the team or to put in the hours that had come to be expected in the role. He played golf every Wednesday and was seen not to add value or to be active in the future plans of the group. The chairman enjoyed the relationship at first – and the opportunity to get deeper into the business.

But Frost was disheartened from very early on. The job was not as described to him during the interview. And he was exasperated by and opposed to the board's decision to dispose of the engineering division, the area he felt most at home in and hoped to improve.

The cosy relationship with the chairman disintegrated, and there were loud public rows.

Despite the obvious signs of problems, the board took no action in the first year. It felt it would lose face if a new appointee was dismissed with a pay-out of two years' salary, as required by his contract. The business deteriorated over 2000-2002, and Frost signed an agreement to go – with two years' pay.

Two years later, the company was taken back into private ownership, for 10 per cent of the share price in 1997 and 40 per cent of the share price when Frost was appointed.

The list of problems that could have a significant impact on the organisation and require immediate action is long. It includes:

- ☐   strategic mishaps resulting in a significant loss of value;

- ☐   disagreements that render the board dysfunctional. (Serious conflict between the CEO and the chairman is the most damaging);

- ☐   appointment of a chief executive who's unsuitable for the organisation and has to be replaced;

- ☐   a failure in the control environment resulting in mis-statement of earnings or fraud;

- ☐   a breakdown in the values of the organisation resulting in a serious complaint – e.g. discrimination;

- ☐   a major health and safety failure resulting in serious injury or death;

- ☐   inability to recruit, retain and motivate people with the required skills to deliver the strategy;

- ☐   a serious product recall or service failure resulting in reputational damage.

There is always the prospect that the board will need to face up to issues like these during a director's term of office. The directors' response to the crisis very much determines the extent of the damage caused.

The first observation is that prevention is better than cure. The approach to governance must be robust; in other words, the theory (the understanding of governance structures) must be matched by what happens in practice.

Ensuring that there is a tight control environment will help to limit the probability of unwelcome events. The application of risk assessment and control, discussed in chapter 5, is an excellent starting point. Small companies can follow the *essence* of the approach without too much of the process detail.

A strong, independent audit committee is integral to the control environment.

There must be clear policies on areas such as health and safety; and processes to ensure that disagreements at board level can be tackled quickly and resolved effectively. The board effectiveness review and the appraisals of individual directors are key elements in keeping the board in good "working order". They are discussed further in chapter 4.

Summary

The role of the board is contained in a set of important principles that directors need to understand. The early part of this chapter reminds the reader of the environment in which the company, a separate legal entity, operates. Directors need to act in the best interests of the company at all times – and this increasingly means having regard to wider issues of good citizenship such as the environment and the interests of the stakeholders.

Because emphasis is placed on the Combined Code as well as legal requirements, much of this chapter strictly applies only to listed companies. However, the principles discussed are good for companies and organisations of all sizes.

Getting the right balance on the board makes decision-making more robust and helps even smaller companies to improve governance.

Directors need to be clear about what is expected of them, and careful consideration needs to be given to the matters reserved for the board.

The statement of matters reserved for the board can be usefully supplemented by a statement of delegated powers to committees of the board or to individuals. The main committees of the board are those set out in the Combined Code – the audit and risk committee, the remuneration committee and the nomination committee. There may also be a case for other special committees such as a treasury and a health and safety committee.

Many boards insist that health and safety is of such paramount importance that it needs to appear on the board agenda at least twice a year.

Board performance is improved by:

☐   annual appraisals for directors;

☐   feedback from the senior non-executive to the chairman;

☐   a formal review of the board's own effectiveness.

Early on, the board needs to decide when and how frequently meetings will be held and the information that should be provided to directors. Most companies recognise that financial information alone is not enough to monitor the health of the business and adopt a form of balanced scorecard.

Even when all the set pieces are in place, there is the possibility that things will go wrong. The board's response is critical in stemming losses or protecting reputation. Choosing the right chief executive will help keep risks to a minimum.

APPENDIX
FOUR KEY TASKS OF THE BOARD
(Summarised from *Standards for the Board*, IoD July 2006)

A. Develop and maintain vision, mission and values

☐ Determine/maintain the company's vision and mission to guide and set the pace for its current operations.

☐ Determine/maintain the values to be promoted throughout the company.

☐ Determine/maintain and review company goals.

☐ Determine/maintain company policies.

B. Develop strategy and structure

☐ Review and evaluate present and future opportunities, threats and risks in the external environment; and current and future strengths, weaknesses and risks relating to the company.

☐ Determine strategic options, select those to be pursued, and decide the means to implement and support them.

☐ Determine the business strategies and plans that underpin the corporate strategy.

☐ Ensure that the company's organisational structure and capability are appropriate for implementing the chosen strategies.

C. Delegate to and monitor management

☐ Delegate authority to and monitor management, and evaluate the implementation of policies, strategies and business plans.

☐ Determine the monitoring criteria to be used by the board.

☐ Ensure the internal controls are effective.

☐ Communicate with senior management.

D. Fulfil responsibilities to shareholders and stakeholders

☐ Ensure that communications both to and from shareholders and stakeholders are effective.

☐ Understand and take into account the interests of shareholders and stakeholders.

☐ Monitor relations with shareholders and stakeholders by gathering and evaluation of appropriate information.

☐ Promote the goodwill and support of shareholders and stakeholders.

the company and the legal duties and liabilities of directors

CHAPTER 2

Introduction

This chapter focuses on some of the main obligations of boards under UK law. For directors of public companies, there may be additional requirements under the Stock Exchange's Listing Rules and the Combined Code on Corporate Governance.

It should be noted that the law does not differentiate between non-executive and executive directors; many of their duties (and therefore their liabilities) will be the same.

The company

As we've seen in the first chapter, a company, as far as the law is concerned, exists in its own right: it is a separate entity from its management and shareholders. There are two very important consequences for directors or those performing the role of director:

☐   they are not liable for the company's debts and cannot, as a general rule, be forced to pay them;

☐   they can be convicted of stealing from their company (even if they own all the shares).

In some companies, liability for debts will be limited by guarantee. Instead of shareholders, there will be guarantors – people who agree to pay a limited sum towards the settlement of debts if the company is wound up. Many charities are **limited by guarantee**.

By far the most common form of company, however, is one where liability is **limited to share capital**, where the shareholders' responsibility for debt cannot exceed the sum they have invested.

There are two important groups with direct financial involvement in the company. First are the shareholders who have put up the risk capital and who have rights that flow from this. In the case of a public company, the shares may be listed on the stock market and traded at prices that reflect its current and expected performance. Second are the creditors who lend money or provide goods and services on credit, and therefore are at risk if the company fails.

In the event of a winding up, assets must, by law, be distributed in a "pecking order". First in line are creditors who have some security attached to particular assets of the company, next are preferential creditors as prescribed by law, then ordinary creditors. Shareholders are last in line and therefore expect a premium to reflect that risk.

Private equity holders

Companies come in a number of forms and are funded in a number of ways. There are small private companies that have a limited number of shareholders, there are family-owned companies, there are quoted companies, with shares traded on a public market such as the AIM or the London Stock Exchange, and there are companies financed partly by high-net-worth individuals or the specialist private equity funds.

Private equity is a common source of capital for small businesses that are starting to expand. It is medium to long-term finance provided in return for an equity stake in potentially high-growth unquoted companies.

It can be used for:

☐ business development plans;

☐ buy outs of existing shareholders by existing management;

☐ buy ins – whereby existing shareholders are bought out and some key managers come into the business.

Private equity is very different from debt finance. Whereas banks and other lenders look for security and have the right to payment of interest and capital ahead of shareholders, private equity holders are investors whose returns are dependent upon the success of the business.

The focus of private equity providers is businesses with good prospects of appreciable growth in sales and profits. They put money on the future performance of a business, and they expect a significant reward for the risk they take. They typically look for an exit route within five years and typically expect returns of 25 per cent to 35 per cent, based on a tax paid internal rate of return (IRR).

Fees are also high as there is usually considerable due diligence before an investment.

The factors that will persuade private equity professionals to invest include:

☐ a credible business plan that sets out clear actions and milestones;

☐ a clear, competitive product or service advantage or unique selling proposition (USP);

☐ a top-class management team with the right balance of skills and, crucially, the right leader;

☐   a hunger for growth;

☐   internal controls that are robust in a growth phase.

Crucially, as far as this book is concerned, **private equity often results in significant change to the way the company is managed**. The private equity provider will usually insist on one or two seats on the board, depending on their level of interest. Where they provide the majority of capital, they may insist on appointing their own nominee as chairman.

There will be greater emphasis on change, cash generation, the exit route to realise their investment and extracting optimum value from the business. The profit and loss account will be examined each month, and the private equity nominee directors will drill down to quite a detailed level to ensure the extraction of value. Pressure will be brought to bear to replace those people who are not performing to the standards required. Unlike owner-managers or founders, private equity professionals will be emotionally detached from the company and will therefore be likely to take a more clinical, pragmatic approach.

Shareholders and stakeholders

Directors are fiduciaries, acting on behalf of shareholders, and a company's purpose is to continue to perform satisfactorily and provide adequate returns for shareholders. (The interests of creditors only take precedence in the event of an insolvency, see page 27.) However, the concept of what the Blair government termed "enlightened shareholder value" means that the interests of shareholders are increasingly seen as linked to those of other groups. These are often called stakeholders and include customers, suppliers, labour, government and the community at large.

It is clear that a company is an **economic organisation** and a major contributor to the wealth of the countries in which it operates. But it is also clear it is a **social organisation**, and this means that decisions may be more complex than first envisaged because non-economic factors need to be taken to account.

The UK Companies Act, supported by case law, makes it clear that directors are to run the company in its best interests and to the benefit of shareholders. But revisions to the Act made in 2006 require directors to take into account in its decisions specified corporate social responsibility factors, enshrining, for the first time, the concepts of the **stakeholder** and **enlightened shareholder value** in UK law.

Directors' duties

For over 250 years, common law has said that directors need to act in good faith and with honesty, and exercise due care and skill in carrying out their duties. Sections 171-177 of the Companies Act 2006 "codify" those duties in a statutory statement. There are seven key legal duties owed by directors. These are summarised in Figure 2.1.

FIGURE 2.1
SEVEN GENERAL DUTIES OF DIRECTORS

☐ To act within the powers of the company

☐ To promote the success of the company for the benefit of its members as a whole, paying due regard in decision-making to: likely long-term consequences; employees' interests; the need to foster relationships with suppliers, customers and others; the impact of operations on the community and the environment; the need to maintain high standards of business conduct and to act fairly between members of the company

☐ To exercise independent judgment

☐ To exercise reasonable care, skill and diligence

☐ To avoid conflicts of interest

☐ Not to accept benefits from third parties

☐ To declare, where applicable, any interest in a transaction or arrangement with the company

---

The general duties will be owed to the company and apply to all directors and shadow directors (those other than professional advisers who exert a material, long-term influence on the board). The powers and rules of the company are set out in the memorandum and articles of association, which place limits on what the company can do.

Directors have a complex role. They are, as Figure 2.1 suggests, required to balance often competing or conflicting demands. Think of the potentially paradoxical statements below.

☐ The board must be entrepreneurial and drive the business forward while keeping it under control.

☐ The board needs to have a clear risk assessment and control process to manage agreed risk, but, at the same time, must be prepared to take calculated risks (profits are, in some part, the rewards of risk-taking).

☐ The board needs to be informed about the workings of the company but must not interfere in the day-to-day management.

☐ The board must be sensitive to short-term issues but remember that its over-riding goal is the creation of long-term value.

☐ The board must be sensitive to local issues but be aware of non-local influences such as macro-market trends, the actions of competitors and supplier opportunities. (Increasingly, trade unions take an international view in their negotiations with companies.)

Record-keeping and other duties

Directors are legally bound to keep proper accounting records and accurate minutes of meetings and to file the required information with Companies House. Although administrative duties are delegated to the company secretary, the ultimate responsibility remains with the board.

There is a plethora of other regulations that affect the company and therefore the directors. Relevant areas of the law include employment, health and safety, the environment, data protection, labelling and consumer rights, taxation and market abuse. In some of these areas, for example, health and safety, breaches may create personal liability for directors.

While almost all companies provide directors' and officers' liability insurance, any serious breach will be a significant cost in terms of reputation – for both organisation and director involved.

If the company is regulated under the **Financial Services and Markets Act 2000 (FSMA)**, there will be specific additional rules. Directors in breach of FSMA will be pursued by the Financial Services Authority (FSA) and can face criminal prosecution and hefty fines.

(Note that insurance policies won't cover fines imposed by either the criminal courts or the FSA.)

Preparation of accounts

Directors must approve both the annual report and accounts and press releases that accompany publicly released information.

The form of the annual report and accounts is prescribed, and copies must be sent to all shareholders and to the registrar of companies. With the permission of individual shareholders, an abbreviated report and accounts can be sent out.

Publication of the report and accounts can be by e-mail or via the company website, provided that intended recipients are informed. A company is legally required to send unabridged hard-copy versions of the annual report and accounts to shareholders who request them.

The period allowed for delivering the report and accounts is within 10 months from the end of the relevant accounting year for a private company and seven months for a public one.

Small and medium companies have some leeway: they can elect by resolution to dispense with the laying of the report and accounts before the shareholders in general meeting. This is also true for subsidiary companies.

Insolvency

In normal circumstances, the accounts are signed off on a "going concern" basis. This means that the directors and the auditor declare they are satisfied that there is sufficient cash resource or facilities to meet the cash requirements of the company for 12 months from the date of signing. Directors will expect to see the evidence of this in the form of forward cash projections, and any assumptions that are made in these projections should be looked at carefully.

Where a company is currently unable to meet its liabilities as they fall due or if the liabilities exceed the assets, the company is deemed insolvent. **Directors may be held personally liable if they continue to trade while the company is insolvent.**

In cases of insolvency, the focus of directors' attention changes. Instead of acting in the best interests of the shareholders in general they must put the interests of creditors first. This means taking all steps possible to avoid loss to creditors. Directors must not act for personal gain or act in a way that gives preference to any creditor, save for those that are properly designated as a preferred creditor in the event of liquidation.

If the company becomes insolvent, the **Insolvency Act** imposes duties and responsibilities on the directors to protect creditors. The effect of these duties is that: *the directors may be liable for* **unlawful trading** *unless they have taken all proper steps to minimise the creditors' losses, once they were aware, or reasonably should have been aware, that there was no reasonable prospect that insolvency could have been avoided.*

Breach of this provision may result in directors being ordered by the court to contribute to the assets of the company and /or disqualification. In addition, there is the possibility of civil action.

All this means that it is essential that directors act with extreme care if their company gets into financial difficulties. They must act objectively rather than recklessly, and they will need to be able to demonstrate that they sincerely believed that there was a reasonable prospect that the company could have avoided insolvent liquidation.

Insolvency and its implications for directors are discussed in detail in chapter 8 of this book's sister publication, *The Director's Handbook*, but in circumstances where there is the prospect of insolvency it is prudent to take professional legal advice.

Disqualification

In addition to civil and criminal liabilities, errant directors can face disqualification for between two and 15 years.

As well as wrongful trading, a director can be disqualified for:

☐   serious or persistent offences in connection with the direction and/or management of the company;

☐   fraud and tax evasion;

☐   failure to file documents with Companies House;

☐   unfit conduct at a company that has, at any time, become insolvent.

Shareholders as well as others, such as creditors, may apply to the court for a disqualification order. If the disqualified director continues to act, they can be imprisoned for up to two years, fined or made personally liable for the debts of the company.

Expectations of directors

We've already seen that directors must operate within the memorandum and articles of their company and not exceed the powers or constraints set out there. Directors must use reasonable skill, care and diligence in carrying out their duties if they are to avoid liability for negligence.

A higher standard of care is expected of directors whose roles require specialist skills and knowledge; the chairman of the audit committee is probably the most obvious example.

Directors need to be present at meetings. Indeed, it is now highly unusual for a director to miss a scheduled board meeting.

There is a requirement for directors to act in good faith and in the best interests of the company, and not place themselves (knowingly or unknowingly) in a position of conflict. These obligations arise from the director's position as a fiduciary – someone who looks after assets on behalf of others.

The word probity probably best sums up the qualities required. The key imperatives are listed in the IoD publication *Standards for the Board* – see Figure 2.2 below. They are expanded further in the Chartered Director Code of Professional Conduct, reproduced at Appendix II.

FIGURE 2.2
EXAMPLES OF THE PROBITY REQUIRED OF DIRECTORS

- ☐ Boards must comply with all relevant laws and regulations
- ☐ Directors must act with integrity
- ☐ Company assets and resources must be applied for proper purposes
- ☐ Directors must exercise their powers in the interests of the company as a whole, not any particular group or individual
- ☐ There should be no conflicts of interest; if they arise, they must be openly reported to the board; no director should be involved in decisions about transactions in which they have a personal interest
- ☐ A director must not seek or obtain gain from their role
- ☐ Inside information must not be used or passed on to others
- ☐ A director must not trade their shares in closed periods or during any time inside information is held

---

Source: *Standards for the Board*, 2006 edition

Summary

Directors have legal responsibilities to shareholders, creditors and to others affected by their activities. This applies irrespective of the size or type of company.

The company will have a written constitution, the memorandum and the articles of association, which lays out what it can and can't do. But it's just part of a vast rulebook. (The Companies Act 2006 is reputedly the longest piece of legislation ever to have been passed by the UK parliament.)

Directors do not need to be legal experts to be effective but they do need to have a working knowledge of the laws that relate to them and their organisations. Those who break the rules face censure, fines and, sometimes, disqualification and imprisonment.

The role of director is challenging; the expected standards increasingly high. But for those who bring the weight of their experience and good judgment to add real value to the company, it is also immensely rewarding.

Directors must act in the best interest of the company at all times. A director's personal reputation and effectiveness depend on their personal standards, as delivered through the consistency of their actions.

governance

CHAPTER 3

Introduction

The subject of governance is a thread that runs throughout this book. The purpose of this chapter is to try to pull together the different strands.

Much of what follows is relevant to any organisation, of any size.

Some first thoughts

The concept of governance is not new; and it did not originate in commercial organisations. Ever since we started living in groups we've needed basic rules for resolving disputes and achieving agreed goals.

The need for rules is arguably greater when groups of people diverge. The separation of labour from ownership in the industrial age led to a concentration of wealth and power in the hands of a few: those at the top of companies. In modern times, the power of some corporations has been much greater than that of some of the countries in which they've operated.

The imbalance of economic power inevitably attracted the attention of law-makers. Governments have set down rules to:

- [ ] maintain competitive markets, using the principles of fair trade;
- [ ] regulate markets that are non-competitive;
- [ ] maintain a balance between capital and labour and protect the rights of workers;
- [ ] ensure investor and public confidence in the capital markets;
- [ ] protect consumers from unsafe products and from fraud;
- [ ] ensure equality of opportunity irrespective of race, religion, sex, disability or sexual orientation;
- [ ] protect the environment.

Law and regulation have not been the only counter-balancing force, though. The growth of the trade union movement, with centralised bargaining for workers, was a major development and an important consideration in much of corporate decision-making. While trade union membership has declined in Britain steadily over the past 30 or so years, it has increased in some other EU member states and is expected to grow in the developing world.

The right of workers to free association is, of course, a fundamental tenet of the International Labour Organisation and it needs to be respected by any company that "offshores" operations.

What is governance?

Dictionary definitions of governance are of limited help. "The art of ruling or governing a place" does not tell a director what they need to do to ensure that value is created and not destroyed.

Perhaps it is more enlightening to see governance as a *system* by which the organisation is directed and controlled.

The imperative for good governance applies across the differing organisational forms, from companies to charities and NPOs.

Good governance moves beyond the box ticking of compliance. It means much more than following the rules of whatever jurisdiction you're operating in. It means adopting a *modus operandi* or a *modus vivendi* that will add value to your organisation.

In other words, governance is a state of mind.

The following are some of the main "windows" on governance:

- [ ] board structure;
- [ ] the internal control environment;
- [ ] internal information;
- [ ] external information and disclosure;
- [ ] performance evaluation and monitoring;
- [ ] succession planning;
- [ ] compensation levels;
- [ ] the treatment of shareholders.

Board structure and independence

As we have seen in chapter 1, the Combined Code is clear on what is required. While it strictly applies only to those companies listed on the London Stock Exchange, it is widely accepted as a blueprint for best boardroom practice.

A summary of the whole of the Code is given in Appendix I to this book. What follows is a summary of some of the main principles for board composition.

☐ The board should have a balance of skills and experiences, and in the case of larger companies, at least half of its members should be independent non-executive directors (see chapter 4 for the Code's definition of "independence").

☐ The role of chairman and chief executive should ideally be separated, with the former running the board, the latter the company. No one person should have unfettered powers of decision-making. *(This means that smaller and family-owned companies, where the roles of chairman and ceo are usually combined, should have the counsel of a non-executive director who will bring independence and balance to the board.)*

☐ There should be a rigorous process for selecting directors, and each director should have a letter of appointment (usually broadened to a contract for the executive directors and, perhaps, the chairman).

☐ All directors should be subject to re-election; the membership of the board should be refreshed to reflect the company's changing needs and to preserve objectivity and independence.

The control environment

An organisation should have a robust system of financial control.

The practice of providing assurance of this differs from organisation to organisation. At the most basic level, a company will have an accountant draw up the annual accounts that need to be filed with Companies House. At the more sophisticated levels, there will be an audit – an inspection of accounts and accounting procedures, and a discussion on the controls.

Some larger companies will have an **internal audit function** where accounting procedures and the risk environment are reviewed as part of an integrated programme relied upon by the external auditor. These companies will also have a competent **audit committee** that will, on behalf of the board, review and form an opinion about the control environment and the high-level risks (see chapter 5 for further information).

Where an audit does take place, the auditor will testify that the client's financial statement is accurate and correctly drawn up. Where it doesn't, they report directly to shareholders and will state that their opinion is not applicable to other parties such as creditors.

Even if there isn't a need for audited accounts, the accounting firm should be encouraged to review the controls in the business and report to the directors on its findings. The directors will then decide whether or not any action is needed.

It's important to stress that risk assessment and control, the foundation of a healthy control environment, cannot be "outsourced": it remains the responsibility of the board, and demands regular attention from both directors and managers. The best leaders in business and in other organisations recognise its inherent value as a tool for effective management. A 2007 survey of Asian financial services by the Economist Intelligence Unit for PricewaterhouseCoopers concluded that "firms will not reap maximum value from risk management unless their culture, organisation, processes and data are all properly aligned". The same observation applies to most other sectors.

It's important, too, to remember that the system for internal control should be comprehensive. The 1998 Turnbull report, annexed to the Code, emphasised the need to think not only of "narrow financial risks" but also those relating to business reputation and the environment. (For some companies, climate change presents a significant business risk.)

Information for the board

As discussed in chapters 1 and 4, the board needs the right information at the right time if it's to do its job properly. The timely flow of clear, useful and accurate information is a governance tool. It enables the board to understand and monitor progress towards strategic objectives and to assess, identify and anticipate risks.

The IoD's *Standards for the Board*, which has been followed by and endorsed by chartered directors (those who hold the institute's professional qualification), emphasises the need for information to support internal control, for information that is:

☐   timely enough for directors to prepare themselves;

☐   informed by recent activities;

☐   sufficient to judge the likelihood of relevant risks;

☐   sufficient to improve the company's ability to reduce the incidence of and impact of risks.

External information disclosure

Governance is an increasingly important criterion in investment decisions. Fund managers do think about the perceived level of governance in the organisation, as we see in the next chapter. Low standards of governance relative to the peer group mean a lower rating and, therefore, a lower market capitalisation.

Since soft measures are thought of as unreliable, some analysts will rely solely on financial performance when rating a company, taking the view that performing as or better than the market expected is a sign of good governance. Others like Deutsche Bank will try for a more pragmatic assessment and will interrogate the published and presented information. This means that annual reports and presentations to analysts and key shareholders need to find a credible way to reflect the state of governance in the company.

The problem is that published information is often sanitised by compliance-driven, risk-averse lawyers, and the essence of the message is lost.

There can be great similarity between published governance statements. Most of the FTSE 100 statements included in annual reports have the same structure and headings. A summary of their main content is included in Figure 3.1 opposite.

Many organisations will publish supporting or additional information on their websites. This will give an excellent insight into the principles by which a company is run.

Cadbury Schweppes was one of the earliest companies to provide information on governance and the values that inform the business. (Its former chairman, Sir Adrian Cadbury, led the first inquiry into corporate governance in the 1990s and his subsequent report formed the basis of the Combined Code.)

Sir Adrian's code of conduct for his own company has been built on and modernised for today's trading by the current top team. I have briefly summarised the published document in Figure 3.2 (see page 38).

FIGURE 3.1
MAIN CONTENT OF THE CORPORATE GOVERNANCE STATEMENT IN ANNUAL REPORT AND ACCOUNTS

☐ The extent to which the company has followed the Combined Code – and the reasons for any non-compliance

☐ The role of the board and how it is governed; changes in board membership during the year; matters reserved for the board and its main committees; the name and duties of the senior independent director

☐ The way the chairman and chief executive operate; their main responsibilities

☐ The work of the board during the year; a list of board meetings and sub-committee meetings and the attendance of directors at each

☐ Induction for new directors; training and development for all directors

☐ How the company communicates with its shareholders; how companies can use the senior independent director if the occasion demands; procedures for informing shareholders of annual meetings or of extraordinary meetings

☐ Notifiable interests of shareholdings in excess of three per cent

☐ A statement about performance evaluations of the board, its committees, the chairman and each director

☐ Individual reports from the chairmen of the main committees

☐ Directors interests if any. *(Details of any director who has a trading relationship with the company are particularly important)*

☐ Internal control and audit; an outline of the responsibilities of the board; the process of identifying and managing significant risks

☐ A statement on internal audit; how the internal audit function operates and the assurance it gives the board

☐ A statement of "going concern"; a declaration that the directors believe that there are sufficient cash resources or facilities to allow the company to operate for the foreseeable future

FIGURE 3.2
CADBURY SCHWEPPES STATEMENT OF BUSINESS PRINCIPLES

Introduction

At Cadbury Schweppes, we take our responsibility and reputation as a good corporate citizen seriously. We are proud of our principles and their effect on how we do business.

This booklet has evolved from our code of conduct and takes into account global standards – such as the International Labour Organisation conventions and the Universal Declaration of Human Rights – as well as cultural and legal best practices from our local markets.

It clearly states our business principles. It shows their impact on everyone involved with Cadbury Schweppes, from the board, the businesses and employees, to consumers, suppliers and business partners.

Todd Stitzer, chief executive officer

John Sunderland, chairman

Our business principles

Our responsibility, as a group, and as individuals, is to:

☐ promote ethical business practices;
☐ respect the environment and communities in which we operate;
☐ assure equal employment opportunities;
☐ value diversity in the workplace;
☐ provide healthy and safe working environments;
☐ respect human rights and trade ethically.

These principles should sit at the heart of our management processes and inform how we work, all over the world. Through them, we can protect and perpetuate the ethical standards that make Cadbury Schweppes a great company – to work for and to work with.

By working together, we can ensure our company maintains its reputation for ethical standards and keeps its promises.

We work together to create brands people love. This is our core purpose.

Our measure of success is the value we create for our shareowners. But we can only maximise this value if we respect our commitment to every one of our stakeholders: shareowners, consumers, customers, colleagues, suppliers and the communities in which we operate.

At Cadbury Schweppes, we are proud of our heritage and its relevance to our current values throughout the world. These inform what we stand for, how we behave, our approach to business and to management.

In our actions we believe in showing integrity and openness.

Summarised from Cadbury Schweppes published information

Monitoring the business

This does not begin and end with financial reporting. In many organisations, monthly reports go beyond the numbers to include all the measures the board has agreed for assessing the health of the business.

The concept of the balanced scorecard is now well understood. It rates performance against strategy and vision, and typically has four dimensions. These are listed below.

- ☐ **Financial** – measures that show what the organisation needs to do to provide the right returns to shareholders.

- ☐ **The customer** – measures of success with customers. (Of course, these are also indicators of financial performance and long-term health.)

- ☐ **Knowledge, or learning and growth in the organisation** – this focuses on the people in the organisation and the changes the organisation needs to make as it moves along its strategic path towards its vision. (Again, this dimension is inter-related with the financials and the long-term health of the business.)

- ☐ **Internal business processes** – those processes a company must excel at if it is to make real progress towards its vision.

Some companies add a further dimension, monitoring the supply base where this is critical to the delivery of the business plan.

Subsets of the four core dimensions include:

- ☐ financial results compared with the plan, with a description of reasons for variances;

- ☐ progress of the business against pre-determined strategic milestones;

- ☐ health and safety issues and standards;

- ☐ progress of significant projects against agreed milestones;

- ☐ evaluation of significant completed capital projects to understand and disseminate lessons learned;

- ☐ debt levels against facilities and banking covenants;

- ☐ audit committee reports, with special reference to reported weaknesses, breaches of standards, or frauds;

- ☐ occasional employee surveys to understand the messages being fed back and how the company needs to respond to be a "best in class" employer;

- ☐ monitoring compliance with the values and ethical leadership set by the board. (While it's difficult to get hard metrics for this, feedback from employees, customers and suppliers will add to the observations directors will make from their site visits);

- ☐ finally, and worthy of a separate discussion, is succession planning.

Succession planning

One of the most important tasks of a board is to ensure that the people in the organisation are in the right jobs, are properly trained and are motivated to perform. Without appropriate management development and succession plans, the structure of governance is doomed to collapse.

Succession planning is as least as important as the strategic planning exercise but it does not always get the same attention. It must be brought to the board; the board must seek assurance it's being handled properly.

The succession of the chief executive is, of course, particularly important. The board must identify the key skills and competencies that are needed for the delivery of the next stage of the organisation's plan. Where the date of the departure of the chief executive is known, there should be an appropriate period of transition. This is discussed in more detail in chapter 1.

Compensation levels

Institutional investor bodies such as the Association of British Insurers (ABI) and the National Association of Pension Funds (NAPF) see the approach to compensation as an important element of governance.

The report by the remuneration committee in the annual report will give a good insight into how remuneration is decided. Investors will look for a balanced package that includes performance-related elements. A director's total ability to earn from salary, annual bonus and long-term incentives will be carefully monitored.

Where shareholder total returns have fallen, especially in relation to the company's peer group, investors find it difficult to understand why top executive directors should be rewarded beyond their salary.

Payments into "top-hat" pension schemes now also come under scrutiny. This is not just because such payments are effectively deferred income: many final salary schemes in the UK have significant deficits when measured against the accounting standard FRS 17.

Compensation should be competitive, aligned with shareholders' interests and not out of line with the peer group. (Benchmarking exercises form an important part of the work of the remuneration committee.)

The typical remuneration report in the annual report and accounts includes the content listed in Figure 3.3 below.

FIGURE 3.3
FORM FOR A TYPICAL REMUNERATION REPORT IN THE ANNUAL REPORT

☐ The members of the committee (the names of all the non-executive independent directors who comprise the committee and the executives who regularly attend meetings)

☐ The role of the committee; its terms of reference (which will usually be published on the company's website)

☐ The names of advisers to the committee

☐ Remuneration policy

☐ Details of incentives and performance criteria, including annual bonus arrangements and long-term incentives

☐ In the case of long-term incentives dependent on how the company performs relative to its peer group, details of the comparator group and its performance

☐ Individual executive directors' interests in bonus shares and options

☐ Pension and life assurance arrangements

☐ Full details of all directors' salaries, bonuses and other remuneration including benefits and increases in pension benefits for the year

☐ Directors' shareholdings

☐ A statement of how non-executive directors' fees are decided

Shareholder treatment

Investors need to be satisfied that all classes of shareholders are treated equally. The interests of one group should not come before those of another. **Minority shareholders must be seen as part of the total group in whose interests the directors act.**

Some companies have differing classes of shares where one class may have a share of the voting that's disproportionate to their economic interests; promoters of the business may hold such rights as a way of controlling the company. This, however, is unacceptable to most investors and is becoming increasingly uncommon in the UK.

Nuts and bolts

There are procedural, everyday elements to organisational good governance. These should be obvious to anyone who's ever been involved in the management of an organisation, at whatever level, but, for the sake of completeness, they're listed here.

☐ The board must be properly constituted and have sufficient staff resources to undertake its duties.

☐ The number of meetings should be sufficient to allow the board to discharge its duties; and meetings must be planned well in advance to ensure that all directors are able to attend.

☐ Agendas should be planned annually so that all important topics are included.

☐ The specific agenda for a meeting should be given out seven days in advance and be properly supported with papers that are clear and concise.

☐ There should be enough time to devote to the items on the agenda; and the time spent on each item should be commensurate with its importance.

☐ Minutes should be complete and accurate, and available within seven days of the meeting.

Going to market

A private company that's expanding or wants to raise new capital may decide to "go public". In the UK, small and medium-sized companies may choose to float on the AIM, the junior market that's relatively light touch in terms of regulation; larger ones may head for the London Stock Exchange, where they'll be bound by the Listing Rules and, of course, the Combined Code.

A company that wants to come to market needs to prepare itself for an Initial Public Offering (IPO), and this could well take the best part of a year.

The groundwork needs to be thorough, and in many cases the existing owner-manager will need to be prepared to change the way they've managed the business. **In other words, the governance of the company will enter a new phase.**

This can be seen in the case study of a real company, called, for the purposes of this book, Holden Services plc.

CASE STUDY: HOLDEN SERVICES PLC

The background

Holden Services (not its real name) was a business services company in the private sector with a controlling shareholder owning 60 per cent. The balance of the shareholding was owned by staff members and other family members.

The company relied upon excellent contacts across the UK, and leveraged these to provide computer-based "processing" solutions to the public sector, mostly at local-authority level, and also to the private sector. In addition, it had a sprinkling of business with large charities.

Its services included payroll, inclusive of pensioner payroll, pension services, human resource back-office systems, council tax demands and collections, and a number of bespoke systems for special clients. The company was an approved implementer of SAP systems and would quote for this business, often winning – in part because of its low overheads and reputation for delivery.

It had annual turnover of £42m and had been expanding at 15 per cent compound annual growth rate over the past three years. It had a pre-tax margin of 17 per cent, and its advisers put its value at around £85m to £100m.

However, for five years, the profit record had been variable with quite large margin swings.

The chief executive, John Holden, attributed this to the costs of winning and implementing new contracts. (His approach was to define what was included in the quote strictly and pitch at low margins, knowing that incremental work nearly always followed, and at very attractive margins. Anything outside the initial contract was charged at the normal rates.)

Holden had founded the business 15 years previously when he'd resigned from a senior position in a large plc. Aged 58, he was a strong manager with firm views on how to run the company. He set high standards for himself and expected the same of others.

The family shareholders were happy with the success to date but, as none of them was now involved in the company, they wanted to crystallise the value of their shareholding. Holden wanted the company to maintain its identity and not be absorbed into a competitor but was also happy to receive the value for his work, and to commit to a two-year contract of employment if the company went to the stock market.

The problem

Holden's advisers reviewed the business and indicated that there would be a 12-month preparation time for a successful public offering. A number of building blocks had to

CASE STUDY: HOLDEN SERVICES PLC (cont)

be in place. These included ensuring the senior management was strong enough to sustain future earnings once Holden stepped down and that there was a plan to develop the most credible internal candidates and consider them alongside anyone from outside. It was noted that a number of the senior people would be quite rich after the flotation and that their subsequent commitment would be in doubt.

The control environment had to be fit for purpose in a public setting, and the general standards of governance had to be high enough for new investors.

The advisers' investigation uncovered areas of weakness that had the potential to derail an IPO. Their main findings are summarised below.

☐ Holden was believed to be autocratic and not good at communicating internally. This had led to a high turnover among the management team. A coterie of only three people had remained loyal. They had been with Holden for an average of 11 years and had adapted to his style. Their holdings in total accounted for 15 per cent of the share capital. Holden, who took virtually all the decisions, would consult these three colleagues but very few others.

☐ The organisational chart was unusual in that Holden was CEO, chairman and sales director (public sector). The other directors headed technical, marketing and sales to the non-public sector, and group services (finance, human resources, legal and secretarial.)

☐ While there were informal meetings of the four directors, and the legal requirements were observed, regular board meetings were not held.

☐ The management information system

produced quarterly results in total terms for the business limited to profit and loss and balance sheet. Supplementary information included debtors, work in progress and contract billing against milestones in the various live contracts.

☐ The control environment was regarded as "fair". Books of account were in place, but there was no accounting manual, no segregation of duties and no procedures for agreeing bids. There were no client profitability accounts as the overall profitability was deemed to be very good.

☐ There was no formal process of risk assessment and control and, indeed, no formal process for creating and leading strategy (directional change was initiated by Holden and communicated, almost in passing, to his directors).

☐ The directors had paid little attention to their fiduciary duties as the group services director ensured compliance with the obligations of reporting.

☐ Salaries were decided by Holden and he also decided what he should be paid.

☐ Staff turnover was unacceptably high due to a lack of motivation: employees saw themselves as paid hands rather than partners in the success of the business. Salary levels were in the upper quartile to try to compensate for this.

☐ The overall philosophy was a focus on customer service and keeping costs well under control.

The programme

It was agreed that the first step was to find an outside person as chairman, someone capable of giving assurance to the City, of working constructively with the CEO and other directors and of providing direction for the IPO to ensure a successful float in 12 months.

The chairman was chosen from a selection of candidates provided by a small firm of search consultants, and the corporate advisers were represented in the selection process.

The division of duties between the chairman and CEO was agreed, and the chairman initiated a search for two additional non-executive directors, one with a background in finance and the City; the other with a background in general management and the service industry.

The new chairman's priority was to mould the board into an effective unit. After some discussion, it was agreed that the board would have only two executive directors, the CEO and the group services director. This not only reflected the abilities of the executive directors but also provided the appropriate balance.

Audit, remuneration and nomination committees were set up and their terms of reference agreed.

The matters reserved for the board were agreed, along with the authority levels for decision-making. Work began on the accounting manual with some outside help.

The CEO was encouraged to have monthly executive meetings to review the business with the appropriate members of his team and to find the right conduit to communicate with the staff beneath this group.

Information for the board was evaluated, and it was agreed that monthly information based on the balanced scorecard should be prepared; and that this information would go to all directors by the 20th of the month following the month being reported upon.

A schedule of eight regular board meetings was prepared and the coverage of all items throughout the year was agreed. Special topics such as strategic review, management development and succession plans, risk assessment and review were built in.

A plan was made for a risk assessment workshop to identify high-level risks.

The accounting firm reviewed current controls and made recommendations for improvement.

The outcome

Putting the programme in place took longer than expected and it was 18 months before the IPO was made. .

That 18 months was an often painful transition, with Holden mourning the "good old days" when he didn't have to bother with all "this process" and had no need to seek agreement to initiatives or "waste time talking about them". There was often a lot of friction between the executives and non executives.

However, mutual respect between the two groups and a strong focus on their mutual goal overcame the issues, and the company did successfully float.

At the time of flotation, the market was volatile, and pricing was lower than had been hoped. Nevertheless, the company had a market capitalisation of £90m, and seven months later breached the £100m mark.

Holden was quick to point out that the transition was of great value. The non-executives helped him and the other directors make better decisions and lifted a lot of the worry from his shoulders.

Today, staff morale is better, helped in part by improved communication and in part by the

---

CASE STUDY: HOLDEN SERVICES PLC (cont)

fact that Holden, before the float, put 10 per cent of his shareholding into an employee share trust, used as a reward for good service.

The lessons

☐ Good governance adds value and is therefore essential for any company planning an IPO.

☐ Better information makes for better decisions.

☐ Multilateral decision-making helps a company spot and act on opportunities

and minimises the risks of strategic failures.

☐ Greater involvement of staff makes for better performance.

☐ Focus on the talent in an organisation helps the board get a better picture of the talent pool and develop it in a more comprehensive way.

☐ A private company considering an IPO needs to plan well in advance and address warning signs that it's not fit to float.

Some final thoughts

It's difficult for anyone now to deny the case for good governance. In-depth research by Deutsche Bank, published in 2004, found a clear link between standards of governance and share-price performance and equity risk among members of the FTSE 350. It concluded that companies with the highest standards of corporate governance and behaviour outperformed those with the lowest in terms of total shareholder returns.

A search on the internet will uncover a number of other studies with the same message.

The principles of and provisions for good governance laid down by the Combined Code, and used as a frame of reference by stock market analysts, are a useful starting point for any board that wants to establish good practice. Organisations in the public sector have used them as the basis for their own codes. (See, for example, the Governance Code of Practice for Universities.)

The challenge for organisations of all types is first to ensure that they are clear about the required standards and that they have clear values that inform their decision-making. They must then find an effective way of communicating this to the public at large.

Governance is a board responsibility; and the board must ensure its standards are properly supported by management. The organisation must live by and live up to its values.

Boards around the world should, at least annually, objectively review their standards of governance.

the role of the chairman and the non-executive directors

CHAPTER 4

Introduction

The Combined Code calls for the separation of the roles of chairman and chief executive. The chairman is the person who leads and runs the board; the chief executive, by contrast, leads and runs the company.

In some organisations, the leader of the board may be known as "the chair". This has the advantage of "gender-neutrality", but I dislike the term. To me, a chair is a piece of furniture – an inanimate and often wooden object; the very antithesis of an effective leader of the board! I prefer the term "chairman" and have stuck to it throughout this book. It should be read as referring to any incumbent in the role – male or female.

Appointment

The chairman is elected by the board and has the same legal duties as other directors. However, given the importance of their role, in public companies they will usually be appointed after a wide professional search by the nomination committee.

It is essential to match the candidate to the specific needs of the company. The first stage is to set out the recruitment criteria. These will include the experience and knowledge desired and the specific competencies that will augment and complement those already on the board.

The skills set of the chief executive will be a particularly important consideration. The chief executive of one FTSE 100 company, for example, was an excellent operations person with good marketing credentials, but was inexperienced in strategy creation and had little direct knowledge of the industry. The company therefore decided to bring in a chairman with good knowledge of the industry and its key participants and with the vision and flair to develop strategy. This was not in the expectation that the chairman would *lead* the strategic process but that they would offer the chief executive the benefit of their experience.

Chairmen are individuals and bring a measure of personal experience and special knowledge to the board, but there are some **general qualities** necessary for the role. Effective chairmen:

☐ have the intellect and ability to grasp complex issues, distil from them the most important elements and identify the areas for decision-making;

☐ show leadership by word and deed;

- [ ] deliver the best from the team of directors, ensuring that each is able to contribute fully;
- [ ] build relationships within the company, the industry and at large in the community;
- [ ] have the integrity to champion the values of the organisation;
- [ ] are challenging of but empathetic towards the executive team;
- [ ] encourage debate and discussion of the key areas, making decision-making more robust and conclusions more satisfactory;
- [ ] are aware of trends and issues in the community;
- [ ] are respected by and known to the financial community.

The chairman's responsibilities

The most fundamental part of the chairman's role is to run board meetings and any special one-off meetings of directors effectively and efficiently. They must also conduct the annual general meeting – and any other public meetings such as an extraordinary general meeting.

In listed companies, their responsibilities will include attendance at the annual and half yearly results meetings, occasional contact with significant shareholders and meeting with advisers and bankers.

The chairman should not stray into the responsibilities of the executive, but they will want to have their finger on the pulse and be informed of and aware of trends and issues early on.

Areas of added value

Chairmen can add value by:

- [ ] ensuring that the board gives the entrepreneurial leadership the company needs – that it has a clear vision, that it sets the direction and the standards by which the company operates;
- [ ] being clear about the roles of chairman and of chief executive and where they divide;
- [ ] ensuring that the board has the right balance of executive to independent non-executive directors and of skills and experience to work effectively.

The chairman will have an appraisal system for the non-executive directors and a succession plan for them that ensures an orderly transition to "new blood" to meet new challenges. They will also pay due regard to the timing of their own departure.

The board, as already stated, needs to work effectively and efficiently. While this starts with its composition, the *chemistry* between members is also important. The chairman will observe the interaction at meetings and will take the necessary action to draw the best from the team.

Information, communication and consultation

The chairman will ensure that the board receives the right information at the right time. At least annually, they will ask the board if the information they receive is clear, in the right form, produced in time to be effective and relevant to the areas that the board needs to monitor.

The importance of a good supply of good information is hard to over-emphasise. The board's role is not just to monitor the executive and ensure compliance with strategy and regulation and the law. It exists to set the objectives and the direction of the organisation; and it must observe the progress towards these goals.

Communication with the stakeholders through annual reports and other publications must be informative, accurate and reflect the values of the company. The chairman's responsibility does not begin and end with their own statement in the annual report: they should be interested in the entire communication.

Last but certainly not least, the chairman has an important role in ensuring that there are development plans to identify the brightest and best talent for promotion and, perhaps, for consideration as future executive directors. The chief executive should consult them during the process of succession planning for the executive team.

Board committees

It is the chairman's responsibility to see that the committees of the board (examined in some detail in the next chapter) are properly constituted, with clear terms of reference, and the right balance of members. Given they have the primary responsibility for board composition, the chairman will normally chair the nomination committee.

They will not chair the other committees, as this is not considered best practice, but they may attend committee meetings at the invitation of the committee chairman. (It's common to see them at remuneration committee meetings; less so, at audit committee meetings.)

When they do attend committee meetings, they must remember their role is not to attempt to control the meeting or indeed to unduly influence it. (This is sometimes a challenge!)

The chairman and the chief executive

The first task is to to be clear about each other's roles and to express this in formal job descriptions. Transparency about their roles and responsibilities will help build trust between the two individuals – and between them and internal and external stakeholders.

With trust, the chairman will be able to act as an informal sounding board for the chief executive before going to the board. The wise chief executive knows that it is best to have a well-prepared chairman, with no surprises sprung at meetings. When things are hidden, when there is a lack of openness, trust breaks down.

There will inevitably be times of friction and disagreement between these two people but their duty is to rise above them and resolve the issue that has caused the conflict. If chairman and chief executive compete with each other they will be unable to act in the best interests of the company.

The style of the two individuals will dictate how and when they communicate. Some will want an hour together each week to provide an update on current issues and to discuss the future plans of the chief executive.

In larger international organisations, they may meet less frequently, but for a longer period – providing the opportunity for a two-way "download".

For any organisation, it's essential that the two individuals at the top meet before a board meeting to discuss the agenda. Such discussions help make sure the meeting is well run and provide the opportunity to share views in good time.

Is there a practical list of items normally discussed between the chairman and the chief executive? While there is no universal template, given the differing styles of working, there are some universal "themes". Set out in Figure 4.1 is a suggested list of headings.

FIGURE 4.1
LIST OF ITEMS NORMALLY DISCUSSED BY THE CHAIRMAN AND THE CHIEF EXECUTIVE BEFORE A BOARD MEETING

Regular items – discussed monthly

☐ Significant items requiring decisions

☐ Comments on current trading compared with expectations

☐ Any sensitive issues that may be commented upon by the board

☐ Warning signs of failure to meet strategic milestones

☐ Organisational changes at the level of senior management and above

☐ Changes in the competitive environment

☐ Major developments affecting customers – e.g. a decline in service levels

Special items – discussed when necessary

☐ Key issues arising from the strategy review; the stages when the chairman and the board should become involved

☐ Mergers and acquisitions, sales of parts of the company and major joint ventures being considered by the executive

☐ Parameters being considered for the annual plan or budget

☐ The key points likely to be included in the appraisal of executive directors and members of the management committee.* (This allows the chairman's comments to be taken on board in advance of the interview.)

☐ The rating to be given to key executives and executive directors

☐ Objectives and personal goals for the top team

☐ The development plans of the top team

☐ Significant changes to the structure of the organisation

☐ Any major projects, especially those involving ICT

☐ Any proposed changes to key advisers

*The chief executive's own appraisal is a key set piece between the two, as is the setting of their objectives and personal goals

The chairman and the senior independent director

When the investment banker Derek Higgs conducted his 2002 review of corporate governance (hot on the heels of the Worldcom and Enron scandals in the US) he said that boards of publicly listed companies should appoint a senior independent director (sometimes know as the "SID") from among their independent non-executives.

The proposal initially caused controversy, with claims that it made governance more cumbersome and weakened the role of chairman, but it was incorporated into the Combined Code. And, as time has moved on, it seems to have been generally accepted.

The principle behind the proposal is that the senior independent director provides a safety valve in times of conflict or in cases where shareholders believe that their concerns may not be brought to the boardroom table.

Where chairman and chief executive act as one and do not communicate fully with shareholders, the senior independent is able to step in and provide a link. Where relations between chairman and chief executive break down, the SID can intervene, identify the issues that have caused the rift and try to build a consensual path back to normality.

Where the best efforts of the senior independent non-executive fail, the non-executive directors may have to rule on the way forward. In extreme cases, one of the two people at the top may need to be replaced.

The non-executive director

Not all non-executives are the same. There is a difference between the non-executive director and the independent non-executive director. The Combined Code sets out a number of tests for independence. A non-executive will, for example, normally "fail" if:

- ☐ they've been appointed by a major shareholder;
- ☐ they hold cross directorships or have significant links with other directors (i.e. they're part of an "old boys'" network);
- ☐ they have close family ties to the business, including ties to its advisers;
- ☐ they receive remuneration and rewards from the company other than their fees or have been an employee of the company within the past five years;
- ☐ their term of office exceeds nine years.

Independent or not, though, the non-executive will, as we've already seen, have the same obligations and the same potential liabilities as the others on the board. **Directors, in other words, are equal under the law.**

The role and responsibilities of non-executives have intensified over recent years and it is crucial that care is taken over their selection. Candidates must be prepared to make the necessary commitment. Effective non-executives do more than turn up to meetings: they make sure they're adequately informed about the issues on the table; they take the time to refresh their skills; they build networks in the company; they keep up with key developments in the organisation.

As chapter 1 made clear, there is a need for balance on the board – both in terms of the number of non-executives to executives and in terms of skills and experience – and this should be a key consideration for nomination committees.

At the same time, it's important to remember that selection is not a one-way street. The chosen candidate will want to do some due diligence of their own. This will include research on the company and its leading people, talking with advisers, reviewing current issues with the chairman and, separately, the company secretary, and, finally, assessing the chemistry at meetings to decide if they will fit in and enjoy the role. New directors will want to feel they can contribute and add value.

Importantly, they will need to be sure they will have the ability to stand back and look at the big picture and avoid getting immersed in management detail. For those coming straight from an executive position, this can be a difficult adjustment.

Key qualities for the non-executive

Non-executives are valued because they have a wider set of experiences that can be brought to bear on issues and decisions in the company. They are best seen as empathetic to management rather than *sympathetic*: they need to be quite challenging in their analysis and evaluation of proposals put to the board. Sometimes, the contribution of a non-executive may be blunted by the style in which the challenge or comment is made. Some have continually reminded the board of the way things are done at their main employer in their executive role, and this is not always helpful.

Are there some key prerequisites for an effective non-executive director? The CIPD website cites 25 skills. This is a comprehensive list, but it is a bit daunting and it will include skills that are not necessarily essential for all non-executives. Here is my list of 10 attributes. (It will be seen to overlap with the key qualities for a chairman, listed above.)

- ☐ The ability to understand issues and to identify the central points requiring boardroom decisions.

- ☐ Sound judgment.

- ☐ The ability to challenge in a constructive way.

- ☐ The ability to influence through clear communication and persuasiveness.

- ☐ Good interpersonal skills and the ability to manage conflict.

- ☐ Forward thinking; the ability to anticipate and be aware of new trends.

- ☐ The ability to think strategically, and to understand the role of risk assessment and control.

- ☐ Financial and commercial skills sufficient to ensure understanding of the organisation's progress against predetermined goals.

- ☐ Integrity and high ethical standards, demonstrated in practice.

- ☐ Self-awareness; a thirst to improve personal knowledge and personal performance.

Appraisal and review

As we've seen in chapter 1, the Combined Code requires chairmen of all listed companies to meet with the non-executive directors separately each year, and the senior independent director to meet with the non-executive directors to appraise the chairman's performance each year.

All directors will want to see that the board operates well, and the tool that most boards use to establish this is an annual board effectiveness review. The review is inevitably a reflection of the performance of the chairman and is often "outsourced" to a consultant or a professional body such as the IoD.

Set out in Figure 4.2 is the list of headings used by a FTSE 100 company in its annual review of effectiveness. The results are consolidated into a report for the board that receives sufficient "airtime" to consider where improvements can be made.

FIGURE 4.2
BOARD EFFECTIVENESS REVIEW – THE KEY ELEMENTS

A. Corporate Strategy
- ☐ Is clearly understood
- ☐ Is understood by the board
- ☐ Is well understood by shareholders and employees
- ☐ Is regularly reviewed and updated to ensure continued appropriateness, support and effectiveness
- ☐ Directors have collectively and individually brought their knowledge and experience to bear in the testing and development of group strategy
- ☐ Strategic options are effectively and systematically evaluated
- ☐ There is an effective and productive process for the review and updating of group strategy

B. Business Principles
- ☐ Are owned and championed by the board
- ☐ Are underpinned by a set of clear and comprehensive group policies, approved by the board
- ☐ Are reviewed annually by the board and updated to ensure continued appropriateness, support and effectiveness
- ☐ Are explicit, unambiguous and practicable
- ☐ Are championed by the executive management group
- ☐ Provide appropriate guidance and motivation for all staff
- ☐ Are effectively communicated to shareholders and other stakeholders

C. Internal Controls and Risk Management
- ☐ There is a clear and comprehensive framework of risk-based internal controls to implement the group policies adopted by the board and thereby manage significant risks
- ☐ Significant risks are effectively identified and evaluated

- ☐ The board effectively assesses and monitors the system of internal controls and the effectiveness with which risk is being managed

D. Shareholders and Stakeholders
- ☐ The group strategy is effectively communicated to shareholders and other stakeholders
- ☐ The board receives sufficient information about the views of shareholders and other stakeholders from relevant external sources

E. Communications
- ☐ The timing, coverage and quality of shareholder and stakeholder communications is appropriate
- ☐ The board communicates effectively with the executive management group
- ☐ The organisation has the resources, skills and experience to manage the key risks and deliver the business plan

F. Organisation and Culture
- ☐ The group culture encourages continuous improvement
- ☐ Performance reporting is adequate and timely and ensures prompt capture of adverse trends
- ☐ Variances from budget are clearly identified and corrective actions are detailed
- ☐ Management performance is regularly and thoroughly reviewed, and rewards or sanctions are executed promptly

G. Succession, Development and Reward
- ☐ There is an appropriate succession management plan for all board and executive management group positions
- ☐ Training and development are encouraged and are focused on the delivery of the business plan

- [ ] The range of rewards is suited to recruiting and retaining qualified, capable and high-quality staff
- [ ] Rewards are structured to focus on short, medium and long-term performance

H. Board Composition

- [ ] The present board membership and composition are the best for the company, given its current needs
- [ ] The range of skills, knowledge and experience is appropriate
- [ ] The process for identifying and recruiting new board members is transparent and appropriate

I. Board Induction and Training

- [ ] There is a comprehensive programme to provide new non-executive directors with an induction to the group
- [ ] Directors are kept up to date with the latest developments in the regulatory and legal environment and how these affect their responsibilities
- [ ] There is a comprehensive training programme for directors to refresh their knowledge and skills

J. Delegation and Accountabilities

- [ ] The matters reserved for the board are appropriate
- [ ] The present range of committees is capable of addressing all areas that should be reviewed on behalf of the board
- [ ] The committee chairmen report appropriate and timely information on their activities to the whole board
- [ ] The board delegates appropriate authority to senior management

K. Board Meetings

- [ ] The agenda includes only what is important

- [ ] Agenda items and presentations are relevant and timely
- [ ] The agenda allows the appropriate amount of time for the discussion of each item
- [ ] The time allowed for each item is appropriately allocated to ensure proper consideration of key issues
- [ ] The schedule of meetings, lunch and dinner allows adequate time for discussion, participation and reflection
- [ ] Meetings are of high quality and are productive with a full and open discussion of issues
- [ ] Board visits to overseas assets are useful and effective

L. Secretariat Service

- [ ] Board papers are received in sufficient time
- [ ] Board papers are sufficiently clear and concise
- [ ] The minutes accurately reflect the substance of the discussions
- [ ] Minutes are distributed in a timely manner
- [ ] Action points from the meetings are properly followed through
- [ ] The board receives appropriate information on the activities of all its committees and sub-committees
- [ ] The board receives timely and comprehensive advice on matters of governance relevant to items of discussion
- [ ] The AGM venue and arrangements are appropriate

M. Other

- [ ] In which area(s) do you believe the board operates most effectively?
- [ ] In which area(s) do you believe the board operates least effectively?

Summary

As the leader of the board, the chairman performs a pivotal role; the effectiveness of the board is a reflection, in large part, of their performance.

It is crucial that the division of responsibilities between chairman and chief executive is clearly defined and that each understands and respects the other's role and objectives. In the best companies, these objectives are shared with the rest of the board. (The case study in chapter 1 of Cosgrove Manufacturing plc is a good example of what happens when things go wrong between chairman and chief executive.) Openness and trust are the foundations of a good working relationship between the two people at the top.

The chairman's role includes ensuring that the agendas are right for each board meeting, and that all directors have the opportunity to express views.

The board needs to provide leadership to the organisation and make sure decisions by management are consistent with strategy. In pre-board meeting discussions with the chief executive, the chairman will be alerted to management proposals where there may be a strategic conflict and where the board may need to say "no".

The success of the board will largely be a function of the quality and diversity of experience and skills of the non-executive directors. Great care should be taken in their appointment and in their annual appraisal to get the best individually and collectively from them.

The senior independent director can be a useful interface between investors and the company, especially where they feel that the chairman has not acted on their concerns. However, there are residual fears that the role marginalises that of chairman. Again, appointing the right person will be crucial.

The board effectiveness review enables boards (and therefore chairmen) to show continuous improvement. It should be carried out in a systematic, structured way.

key committees
of the board

CHAPTER 5

Introduction

The major and prescribed committees of the board are the audit, remuneration and nomination committees.

This chapter looks at the work of all three, but it examines the audit committee, which is integral to the control environment, in most detail.

Each committee should have clear terms of reference, reviewed annually by the board to ensure their relevance.

The remuneration committee

The basic principle here is that no director should decide their own remuneration.

Non-executive fees are set by the executive directors, often on the advice of external consultants, and are usually paid in cash. (Although some companies will pay part or all of the remuneration in shares.) The remuneration of executive directors is set by a committee of non-executives and will include performance-related elements.

Best practice says that the remuneration committee (or "remco" as it's sometimes known) should be made up entirely of independent non-executive directors and be led by someone other than the chairman of the main board.

Committee meetings are usually attended by the human resources director and, often, the managing director. (Executives should, though, be excluded from discussions in which they have a direct personal interest.) The company secretary usually provides the secretarial back up. Normally, the committee will meet three times a year.

The remuneration committee is encouraged to have independent input on salaries, deferred income such as pensions, and incentives. **In setting rewards, the key rule is to avoid paying more than is necessary to attract, retain and motivate executive talent.** Packages should be competitive and aligned with the delivery of the strategy. The Combined Code calls for a "significant proportion" of performance-related elements, but the precise ratio of base salary to "money at risk" – e.g. annual bonus and longer term plans – will differ from company to company.

The members of the remuneration committee will seek objective assessment of competitors' pay from surveys and consultants. They should, however, think about their company's position in any comparator group carefully. Remuneration policy should not be driven by "me-tooism". Committee members should, says the Code, avoid an "upward ratcheting" in executive pay without a corresponding improvement in performance.

Challenges faced by the remuneration committee

The key challenges are to:

- ensure that the remuneration policy is aligned with the requirements of strategy, is competitive and motivating;
- ensure that the remuneration package is affordable, not excessive and not damaging to the reputation of the company;
- ensure that the remuneration policy is aligned with the interests of shareholders in delivering value;
- avoid rewards for failure.

There has been some debate as to whether the current pay model is fit for purpose. Incentive payments often reward the executive when share prices move up but fail to penalise them when they move down. Currently, executive directors in listed companies do not have significant investments at risk in the companies they run. The private equity model, on the other hand, requires the executive to invest at current prices into the company at levels usually around one or two times salary. Executives with a lot to lose are arguably more motivated to do well.

The remuneration committee will want to ensure that there's a system for effective appraisals against objectives and that targets for bonuses are seen to be stretching but achievable.

The committee needs to identify the population it will look at individually. This will usually include directors of significant subsidiaries, members of the top executive committee and those who have breached a pre-determined income threshold.

The chairman of the committee is responsible for the remuneration report, included in the annual report and accounts, and must be available at the company AGM to answer questions on remuneration.

The importance of getting remuneration right cannot be over-emphasised. Shareholders have the right to an advisory vote on the remuneration report; and "no" votes always attract adverse publicity.

Remuneration committee terms of reference

The Combined Code requires the terms of reference for the defined committees to be formally laid down. Set out in Figure 5.1 are the terms of reference for the remuneration committee of Scottish & Newcastle, a FTSE 100 company.

FIGURE 5.1
TERMS OF REFERENCE – REMUNERATION COMMITTEE, SCOTTISH & NEWCASTLE PLC

Membership

Members of the committee are appointed by the board, on the recommendation of the nomination committee in consultation with the chairman of the remuneration committee. The committee is made up of at least three members, all of whom are independent non-executive directors.

Only members of the committee have the right to attend committee meetings. However, other individuals such as the chairman of the board, the chief executive, the head of human resources and external advisers may be invited to attend for all or part of any meeting as and when appropriate.

The board appoints the committee chairman, who is an independent non-executive director. In the absence of the committee chairman and/or an appointed deputy, the remaining members present elect one of themselves to chair the meeting. The chairman of the board may not be chairman of the committee.

The current members of the committee are: *Names are inserted here*

Secretary

The company secretary or his or her nominee acts as the secretary of the committee.

Quorum

The quorum necessary for the transaction of business is two.

Meetings

The committee meets four times a year and at such other times as are appropriate.

Notice of Meetings

Meetings of the committee are convened by the secretary of the committee at the request of any of its members. Unless otherwise agreed, notice of each meeting confirming the venue, time and date, together with an agenda of items to be discussed, are forwarded to each member of the committee and any other person required to attend, no later than three working days before the date of the meeting. Supporting papers are sent to committee members and to others as appropriate, at the same time or as soon as practicable thereafter.

Minutes of Meetings

The secretary minutes the proceedings and resolutions of all committee meetings, including the names of those present and in attendance.

Minutes of committee meetings are circulated promptly to all members of the committee and, once agreed, to all members of the board, unless a conflict of interest exists.

Annual General Meeting

The chairman of the committee attends the annual general meeting prepared to respond to any shareholder questions on the committee's activities.

Duties

The duties of the committee are to:

- determine and agree with the board the framework or broad policy for the remuneration of the company's chief executive, chairman, the executive directors, members of the executive management group and such other members of the executive management as it is designated to consider. The remuneration of non-executive directors is a matter for the chairman and the executive members of the board. No director or manager is involved in any decisions as to his or her own personal remuneration;

- in determining such policy, take into account all factors that it deems necessary. The objective of such policy shall be to ensure that members of the executive management of the company are provided with appropriate incentives to encourage enhanced performance and are, in a fair and responsible manner, rewarded for their individual contributions to the success of the company;

- review the ongoing appropriateness and relevance of the remuneration policy;

- approve the design of, and determine targets for, any performance-related pay schemes operated by the company and approve the total annual payments made under such schemes;

- review the design of all share incentive plans for approval by the board and shareholders. For any such plans, determine each year whether awards will be made, and if so, the overall amount of such awards, the individual awards to executive directors and other senior executives and the performance targets to be used;

- review the ongoing administration and appropriateness of all share-based remuneration;

- determine the policy for, and scope of, pension arrangements for each executive director and other senior executives;

- ensure that contractual terms on termination (in the case of executive directors, the committee is to approve the amount of any payments made to ensure that they meet these criteria) are fair to the individual, and the company, that failure is not rewarded and that the duty to mitigate loss is fully recognised;

- within the terms of the agreed policy and in consultation with the chairman and/or chief executive as appropriate, determine the total individual remuneration package of each executive director and each member of the executive management group including bonuses, incentive payments and other share awards;

- in determining such packages and arrangements, give due regard to any

FIGURE 5.1 (CONT)
TERMS OF REFERENCE – REMUNERATION COMMITTEE, SCOTTISH & NEWCASTLE PLC

relevant legal requirements, the provisions and recommendations in the Combined Code and the UK Listing Authority's Listing Rules and associated guidance;

☐ review and note annually the remuneration trends across the group;

☐ oversee any major changes in employee benefits structures throughout the group;

☐ agree the policy for authorising claims for expenses from the chief executive and chairman;

☐ ensure that all provisions regarding disclosure of remuneration including pensions, as set out in the Directors' Remuneration Report Regulations 2002 and the Combined Code, are fulfilled; and

☐ be exclusively responsible for establishing the selection criteria and the terms of reference for any remuneration consultants who advise the committee, for appointing consultants and for obtaining reliable, up-to-date information about remuneration in other companies. The committee shall have full authority to commission any reports or surveys that it deems necessary to help it fulfil its obligations.

Reporting Responsibilities

The committee chairman reports formally to the board on its proceedings after each meeting.

The committee makes whatever recommendations to the board it deems appropriate on any area within its remit where action or improvement is needed.

The committee produces an annual report of the company's remuneration policy and practices that forms part of the company's annual report and ensures each year that it is put to shareholders for approval at the AGM.

Other

The committee, at least once a year, reviews its own performance, constitution and terms of reference to ensure it is operating at maximum effectiveness and recommends any changes it considers necessary to the board for approval.

Authority

The committee is authorised:

☐ to seek any information it requires from any employee of the company in order to perform its duties; and

☐ in connection with its duties, to obtain, at the company's expense, any legal or other professional advice.

The nomination committee

This committee leads the process of selecting new board members, making recommendations or nominations to the full board. It will typically also ensure that succession plans are in place for the board and the executive level immediately below it.

It is made up mainly of independent non-executive directors. The chairman of the main board is usually a key member and often chairs the committee (unless its main business is to appoint his or her successor).

In smaller companies, the duties and responsibilities of the nomination and the remuneration committee may be combined.

Figure 5.2 sets out a model terms of reference used by a FTSE 100 company.

The audit committee

The Combined Code says that the audit committee should be comprised of at least three non-executive directors, one of whom should have recent and relevant financial experience.

Current European proposals go further, suggesting that members should have accounting or auditing experience. For the time being in the UK, though, numeracy (financial literacy), good experience and good judgment can be enough to get you a seat. (Critics say the EU proposals define membership too narrowly and would exclude many people capable of making an excellent contribution to the committee.)

The finance director and the head of internal audit will always be in attendance, and the secretary is usually the company secretary or the head of internal audit.

It's usual for the committee to meet quarterly. Naturally, two meetings will coincide with the publication of half-year and full-year results. Additional special meetings are held as necessary.

The scope of the audit committee

The role of the audit committee is commonly misunderstood. The quotes below were all recorded in a straw poll of small investors conducted by the author for a private seminar.

FIGURE 5.2
TERMS OF REFERENCE – NOMINATION COMMITTEE, FTSE 100 COMPANY

Membership

Members of the committee are appointed by the board. The committee is made up of least three members, the majority of whom should be independent non-executive directors.

Only members of the committee have the right to attend committee meetings. However, other individuals such as the chief executive, the head of human resources and external advisers may be invited to attend for all or part of any meeting as and when appropriate.

Appointments to the committee are for a period of up to three years, which may be extended for two further three-year periods provided that the majority of the committee members remain independent.

The board appoints the committee chairman, who should be either the chairman of the board or an independent non-executive director. In the absence of the committee chairman and/or an appointed deputy, the remaining members present elect one of their number to chair the meeting. The chairman of the board does not chair the committee when it is dealing with the matter of succession to the chairmanship.

The current members of the committee are: *Names are inserted here*

Secretary

The company secretary or his or her nominee acts as the secretary of the committee.

Quorum

The quorum necessary for the transaction of business is two, both of whom must be independent non-executive directors.

Frequency of Meetings

The committee meets at least twice a year and at such other times as the chairman of the committee shall require.

Notice of Meetings

Meetings of the committee are convened by the secretary of the committee at the request of any of its members.

Unless otherwise agreed, notice of each meeting confirming the venue, time and date, together with an agenda of items to be discussed, is forwarded to each member of the committee, and any other person required to attend, no later than three working days before the date of the meeting. Supporting papers are sent to committee members and to other attendees as appropriate, at the same time or as soon as practicable thereafter.

Minutes of Meetings

The secretary minutes the proceedings and resolutions of all meetings of the committee, including the names of those present and in attendance.

Minutes of committee meetings are circulated promptly to all members of the committee and the chairman of the board and, once agreed, to all other members of the board, unless a conflict of interest exists.

Annual General Meeting

The chairman of the committee attends the annual general meeting prepared to respond to any shareholder questions on the committee's activities.

Duties

The committee:

- regularly reviews the **structure, size and composition (including the skills, knowledge and experience)** required of the board compared with its current position and makes recommendations to the board with regard to any changes;

- gives full consideration to succession planning for directors in the course of its work, taking into account the challenges and opportunities facing the company, and what skills and expertise are therefore needed on the board in the future;

- is responsible for identifying and nominating, for the approval of the board, candidates to fill board vacancies as and when they arise;

- before making an appointment, **evaluates the balance of skills, knowledge and experience on the board** and, in the light of this evaluation, prepares a description of the role and capabilities required for a particular appointment.

- in identifying suitable candidates, uses open advertising or the services of external advisers to facilitate the search, considers people from a wide range of backgrounds and on merit and objective criteria, taking care that appointees have enough time to devote to the position;

- keeps under review the leadership needs of the organisation, both executive, non-executive and senior management, with a view to ensuring the continued ability of the organisation to compete effectively in the marketplace. In doing so, it will review management development programmes and the succession planning process for the executive management group and other senior management prepared by the chief executive;

- ensures that on appointment to the board, non-executive directors receive a formal letter of appointment setting out clearly what is expected of them in terms of time commitment, committee service and involvement outside board meetings.

The committee also makes recommendations to the board concerning:

- plans for succession for both executive and non-executive directors and in particular for the key roles of chairman and chief executive;

- suitable candidates for the role of senior independent director;

FIGURE 5.2 (CONT)
TERMS OF REFERENCE – NOMINATION COMMITTEE, FTSE 100 COMPANY

- membership of the audit and remuneration committees, in consultation with the chairmen of those committees;
- the re-appointment of any non-executive director at the conclusion of their specified term of office, having given due regard to their performance and ability to continue to contribute to the board in the light of the knowledge, skills and experience required;
- the re-election by shareholders of any director under the "retirement by rotation" provisions in the company's articles of association, having due regard to their performance and ability to continue to contribute to the board in the light of the knowledge, skills and experience required;
- any matters relating to the continuation in office of any director at any time, including the suspension or termination of service of an executive director as an employee of the company, subject to the provisions of the law and their service contract; and
- the appointment of any director to executive or other office (except that of chairman and chief executive, the recommendation for which would be considered at a meeting of the full board).

Reporting Responsibilities

The committee makes whatever recommendations to the board it deems appropriate on any area within its remit where action or improvement is needed.

The committee makes a statement in the annual report about its activities and the process used to make appointments and offers an explanation if external advice or open advertising has not been used.

Other

The committee, at least once a year, reviews its own performance, constitution and terms of reference to ensure it is operating at maximum effectiveness and recommends any changes it considers necessary to the board for approval.

Authority

The committee is authorised:

- to seek any information it requires from any employee of the company in order to perform its duties; and
- in connection with its duties, to obtain, at the company's expense, outside legal or other professional advice.

"It is there to ensure that published accounts are correctly drawn up."

"The audit committee is a vehicle to prevent fraud."

"The audit committee is there to keep management on their toes."

"It gives shareholders assurance that controls in the organisation are robust."

"It is there to comply with the Combined Code."

While there is some element of truth in these views, they do not accurately reflect the work of the committee.

The scope of the audit committee is laid down in its terms of reference and is usually quite wide. Typically, it includes:

☐ providing a direct link with the auditor;

☐ approving the annual internal audit and external audit plan;

☐ ensuring the auditor's independence and agreeing terms under which the audit firm can accept non-audit work;

☐ appraising the auditor's effectiveness;

☐ having a direct reporting relationship with the head of the internal audit function;

☐ reviewing and monitoring the control environment, and in particular ensuring that an appropriate risk assessment and control process is **embedded in the business**;

☐ reviewing and agreeing any changes in accounting policy;

☐ scrutinising the accounts and financial reports to shareholders and, if satisfied, recommending them to the board for approval.

The chairman of the committee must, of course, attend the AGM to answer any questions put to him or her by the shareholders.

The terms of reference show clearly the scope of the audit committee, but the question audit committees need to ask is: **"How can we add value to the organisation?"**

The basic tasks that need to be undertaken are compliance-driven, involving the review of accounts and financial statements, and controls. The broader focus is risk assessment and control, the very foundation for internal and external audit. By playing a fundamental role in the control environment, the audit committee can bring real value and help the organisation meet its strategic goals.

The audit committee and risk assessment

Risks are an inherent part of business life; profits are, to some extent, the rewards of taking risks.

Assessing the risks of a company strategy is now a well-defined procedure, most usefully tackled through risk workshops. Risks are evaluated for impact and probability, and ranked accordingly.

The audit committee needs to satisfy itself that the process of evaluation is robust and that the high-level risks are being identified. High-level risks need to be "owned"; there should be a person responsible for managing each one.

Risk management is not an annual and financial exercise but **an approach that needs to be embedded in the business**. In a 2006 report, the accountants and management consultants Ernst and Young defined it as "a systematic and structured way of aligning an organisation's approach to risk and its strategy, helping the business to manage uncertainty more effectively, to minimise threats and maximise opportunity".

External stakeholders want assurance that the organisation's leaders have the right systems, people and information to reduce exposure to risks and to realise value.

Effective directors are not constitutionally risk-averse; but they're not reckless either.

Terms of reference

Again, the terms of reference need to be formally set down and annually reviewed and approved. Figure 5.3 sets out the terms used by Scottish & Newcastle.

FIGURE 5.3
TERMS OF REFERENCE – AUDIT COMMITTEE, SCOTTISH & NEWCASTLE PLC

Membership

Members of the committee are appointed by the board, on the recommendation of the nomination committee in consultation with the chairman of the audit committee. The committee is made up of at least three members.

All members of the committee are independent non-executive directors, at least one of whom has recent and relevant financial experience. The chairman of the board may not be a member of the committee.

Only members of the committee have the right to attend committee meetings. However, other individuals such as the chairman of the board, group chief executive, group finance director, other directors, the head of group review and audit, and representatives from the finance function may be invited to attend all or part of any meeting as and when appropriate.

The external auditors are invited to attend meetings of the committee regularly.

Appointments to the committee are for a period of up to three years, which may be extended for two further three-year periods, provided the director remains independent.

The board appoints the committee chairman, who is an independent non-executive director. In the absence of the committee chairman and/or an appointed deputy, the remaining members present elect one of themselves to chair the meeting.

The current members of the committee are: *Names are inserted here*

Secretary

The company secretary or their nominee acts as the secretary of the committee.

Quorum

The quorum necessary for the transaction of business is two.

Frequency of Meetings

The committee meets at least four times a year at appropriate times in the reporting and audit cycle and otherwise as required.

Notice of Meetings

Meetings of the committee are convened by the secretary of the committee at the request of any of its members or at the request of any of those individuals referred to above or external auditors if they consider it necessary.

Unless otherwise agreed, notice of each meeting confirming the venue, time and date, together with an agenda of items to be discussed, is forwarded to each member of the committee and any other person required to attend, no later than three working days before the date of the

FIGURE 5.3 (CONT)
TERMS OF REFERENCE – AUDIT COMMITTEE, SCOTTISH & NEWCASTLE PLC

meeting. Supporting papers are sent to committee members and to others as appropriate, at the same time or as soon as practicable thereafter.

Minutes of Meetings

The secretary minutes the proceedings and resolutions of all meetings of the committee and records the names of those present.

The secretary ascertains, at the beginning of each meeting, the existence of any conflicts of interest and minutes them accordingly.

Minutes of committee meetings are circulated promptly to all members of the committee and, once agreed, to all members of the board.

Annual General Meeting

The chairman of the committee attends the annual general meeting prepared to respond to any shareholder questions on the committee's activities.

Duties

The committee should carry out the duties below for the parent company, major subsidiary undertakings and the group as a whole, as appropriate.

Financial Reporting

The committee monitors the integrity of the financial statements of the company, including its annual and interim reports,

preliminary results announcements and any other formal announcement relating to its financial performance, reviewing any significant financial reporting issues and judgments that they contain. The committee also reviews summary financial statements, significant financial returns to regulators and any financial information contained in certain other documents, such as announcements of a price-sensitive nature.

The committee reviews and challenges where necessary:

- [ ] the consistency of, and any changes to, accounting policies both on a year-on-year basis and across the company/group;

- [ ] the methods used to account for significant or unusual transactions where different approaches are possible;

- [ ] whether the company has followed appropriate accounting standards and made appropriate estimates and judgments, taking into account the views of the external auditor;

- [ ] the clarity of disclosure in the company's financial reports and the context in which statements are made;

- [ ] the treatment of any items in the financial statements that differs from the views of the company's external auditor;

- [ ] the going concern assumption; and

- [ ] all material information presented with the financial statements, such as the business review and the corporate governance statement (insofar as it relates to audit and risk management);

Internal Controls and Risk Management Systems

The committee:

- keeps under review the effectiveness of the company's internal controls and risk management systems; and

- reviews and approves the statements to be included in the annual report concerning internal controls and risk management.

Whistleblowing

The committee reviews the company's arrangements for its employees to raise concerns, in confidence, about possible wrongdoing in financial reporting or other matters. The committee ensures that these arrangements allow proportionate and independent investigation of such matters and appropriate follow-up action.

Internal Audit

The committee:

- monitors and reviews the effectiveness of the company's group review and audit in the context of the company's overall risk management system;

- approves the appointment and removal of the head of group review and audit;

- considers and approves the remit of group review and audit, ensures it has adequate resources and appropriate access to information to perform its function effectively and in accordance with the relevant professional standards, and ensures it has adequate standing and is free from management or other restrictions;

- reviews and assesses the annual internal audit plan;

- reviews promptly all reports on the company from the internal auditors;

- reviews and monitors management's responsiveness to the findings and recommendations of group review and audit; and

- meets the head of group review and audit at least once a year, without management being present, to discuss their remit and any issues arising from the internal audits carried out. In addition, the head of group review and audit has the right of direct access to the chairman of the board and to the committee.

External Audit

The committee:

- considers and makes recommendations to the board, to be put to shareholders for approval at the AGM, in relation to the appointment, re-appointment and removal of the company's external

FIGURE 5.3 (CONT)
TERMS OF REFERENCE – AUDIT COMMITTEE, SCOTTISH & NEWCASTLE PLC

auditor. The committee oversees the selection process for new auditors and if an auditor resigns the committee investigates the issues leading to this and decides whether any action is required;

☐ oversees the relationship with the external auditor, including (but not limited to):

approval of its remuneration, whether fees for audit or non-audit services, ensuring that the level of fees is appropriate to enable an adequate audit to be conducted;

approval of its terms of engagement, including any engagement letter issued at the start of each audit, and the scope of the audit;

assessing annually its independence and objectivity, taking into account relevant professional and regulatory requirements and the relationship with the auditor as a whole, including the provision of any non-audit services;

satisfying itself that there are no relationships (such as family, employment, investment, financial or business) between the auditor and the company (other than in the ordinary course of business);

monitoring the auditor's compliance with relevant ethical and professional guidance on the rotation of audit partners, the level of fees paid by the company compared with the overall

fee income of the firm, office and partner, and other related requirements;

assessing annually the auditor's qualifications, expertise and resources, and the effectiveness of the audit process, which shall include a report from the external auditor on their own internal quality procedures; and

developing and implementing a policy on the supply of non-audit services by the external auditor, taking into account any relevant ethical guidance on the matter.

☐ meets regularly with the external auditor, including once at the planning stage before the audit and once after the audit at the reporting stage. The committee also meets the external auditor at least once a year, without management being present, to discuss its remit and any issues arising from the audit;

☐ reviews and approves the annual audit plan and ensures that it is consistent with the scope of the audit engagement;

☐ reviews the findings of the audit with the external auditor. This shall include but not be limited to, the following:

a discussion of any major issues that arose during the audit;

any accounting and audit judgments;

levels of errors identified during the audit; and

a discussion of the treatment of any item in the financial statements that differs from the views of the external auditors.

- ☐ reviews any representation letter(s) requested by the external auditor before they are signed by management;

- ☐ reviews the management letter and management's response to the auditor's findings and recommendations;

- ☐ reviews the effectiveness of the audit.

Reporting Responsibilities

The committee chairman reports formally to the board on its proceedings after each meeting. The committee makes whatever recommendations to the board it deems appropriate on any area within its remit where action or improvement is needed. The committee compiles a report to shareholders on its activities to be included in the company's annual report.

Other Matters

The committee:

- ☐ has access to sufficient resources in order to carry out its duties, including access to the company secretariat for assistance as required;

- ☐ is provided with appropriate and timely training, both in the form of an induction programme for new members and on an ongoing basis for all members;

- ☐ gives due consideration to laws and regulations, the provisions of the Combined Code and the requirements of the UK Listing Authority's Listing Rules;

- ☐ is responsible for co-ordination of group review and audit and external auditors;

- ☐ oversees any investigation of activities that are within its terms of reference and acts as a court of the last resort; and

- ☐ at least once a year, reviews its own performance, constitution and terms of reference to ensure it is operating at maximum effectiveness and recommends any changes it considers necessary to the board for approval.

Joint Ventures and Associated Companies

Where the group has investments in joint ventures or associated companies that do not confer control, the committee reviews, so far as practicable, the arrangements relating to the duties described above.

Authority

The committee is authorised:

- ☐ to seek any information it requires from any employee of the company in order to perform its duties;

- ☐ to obtain, at the company's expense, outside legal or other professional advice on any matter within its terms of reference; and

- ☐ to call any employee to be questioned at a meeting of the committee as and when required.

Improving audit committee effectiveness

The audit committee will periodically review how it can be more effective and add greater value to the enterprise; it will continuously seek to improve its performance.

An important tool for achieving continuous improvement is an annual review of effectiveness. This can be carried out in several ways:

☐ by having a detailed questionnaire that is agreed with the chairman of the committee and circulated to committee members, members of the senior

---

FIGURE 5.4
DRAFT QUESTIONNAIRE, AUDIT AND RISK COMMITTEE, INSTITUTE OF DIRECTORS

1. Terms of Reference

☐ Has the committee clear, approved terms of reference?

☐ Are these reviewed annually?

☐ Is there a clear policy on whistle-blowing?

☐ Is there clarity on the engagement of the auditors for non-audit work?

2. Membership and Appointments

☐ Does the audit committee consist of independent members?

☐ Are members appointed by the board, or the nomination committee, in consultation with the audit committee chairman?

☐ Does at least one member have recent and relevant experience?

☐ Is there a relevant balance of skills on the committee?

☐ Are terms of office restricted to three years?

☐ Does the committee have succession plans?

☐ Is there an induction programme for new members?

☐ Do members take steps to update their knowledge and skills?

3. Meetings

☐ Does the committee meet regularly and at least three times a year?

☐ Are the meetings well attended?

☐ Is sufficient time allowed for discussion?

☐ Are agendas prepared well, with relevant information, and on time?

☐ Are arrangements made for the committee to meet alone with the auditors?

☐ Does the chairman keep in touch with key staff and the audit partner?

☐ Are appropriate non-members invited and encouraged to attend?

☐ Is the committee adequately served by the staff?

4. Review of Accounts

☐ Does the committee review all significant financial reporting issues and judgments made?

☐ Where there is a difference of view between the auditors and the IoD does the committee formally consider what is appropriate?

☐ Is there a committee review of the clarity and completeness of statements?

☐ If there is any significant aspect of

executive team, other board members and the partner of the audit firm;

☐ by having an independent qualified person carry out structured interviews;

☐ by having the audit firm review the committee, using external best practice as its benchmark.

In each case, the "results" are consolidated and actions agreed to improve performance.

Figure 5.4 reproduces the questionnaire devised for the audit and risk committee of the IoD.

disagreement with the accounts are changes made, or is this reported to the board?

☐ Does the committee review any significant differences between accounts produced by the IoD and the auditors' workings?

5. Internal Controls and Risk Assessment

☐ How well is risk assessment embedded in the IoD?

☐ Does the committee have a list of high-level risks?

☐ How well are the risks managed at the IoD?

☐ Does the committee monitor the integrity of the controls?

☐ Is the committee satisfied that the information available to the board enables it to monitor the business effectively?

☐ Is the annual assessment made on establishing an internal audit function?

6. External Auditor

☐ Is the committee responsible for overseeing the auditor?

☐ Does the committee recommend the appointment or removal of the auditor?

☐ Is the annual auditor's work plan agreed by the committee?

☐ Does the committee monitor the skills and independence of auditors?

☐ Is the committee aware of the auditor's processes to preserve quality and independence?

☐ Has a level of materiality been agreed with the auditors?

☐ Does the committee monitor the management letter and ensure that follow-up is timely and appropriate?

☐ Is there a formal review of the effectiveness of the audit?

7. Other Matters

☐ Are copies of the minutes distributed to members and to the board promptly?

☐ Does the report of the committee go to the board?

☐ Is the chairman of audit available at IoD council meetings/the AGM?

8. Finally ...

☐ What does the committee do really well?

☐ What areas must be improved to achieve best practice?

☐ Are there areas you are concerned about because you see the IoD at risk?

The audit committee and relationship-building

The role of the chairman of the committee is pivotal. He or she can build trust between the committee and the auditor, the internal audit team, the finance director and the key general managers of the main businesses including the CEO. A spirit of openness is essential for effective working: no party should surprise another.

The committee chairman needs to make the time to maintain the important relationships in the company, to keep up-to-date with changes in accounting and auditing standards, and to support and interact with the internal audit leader and team.

Chairing an audit committee is thus a difficult task that places significant demands on an individual. The Smith Guidance on audit committees, annexed to the Combined Code, says this should be reflected in the chairman's remuneration.

The audit committee's understanding of the business is enhanced by presentations from executives that focus on the control environment, and, perhaps, significant organisational change. Specific areas to consider include:

- tax strategy;
- foreign exchange hedging policy;
- the risk assessment and control process;
- an evaluation of past capital projects.

This last exercise is a valuable one for the business as it looks at significant capital expenditure and compares the out-turn with what had been planned. It is not just another financial exercise: it will reveal strengths and weaknesses in project management and help build a bank of knowledge to improve decision-making. It's vital that lessons are learned from the process. Again, a spirit of openness will be helpful: executives should face up to honest mistakes; this is not the time for self-justification or defensiveness.

The internal audit team will have an annual approved work plan for the year ahead. Audit reports are shared with the audit committee, and dates are agreed for implementing recommendations.

The audit committee can learn a lot from the organisation's responses to the recommendations. Defensiveness may point to further weaknesses in the control environment.

Agreed actions should be monitored by the committee and, where important recommendations have not been implemented to time, the executives concerned should be called to account.

The internal audit plan should complement work by the external auditor so that duplication is avoided and so that the external auditor can rely on work by the internal auditor.

Risk assessment and control

As we've already seen, the audit committee must ensure that there is a process that:

- identifies the risks in the business;
- evaluates their impact;
- assesses the probability of the event happening;
- grades the risks.

The high-level risks are reviewed by the audit committee and the board, and a plan is developed to manage and thereby ameliorate them.

The process works well when there is a "bottom up" approach in the trading divisions or separate companies and then a "top down" approach from the executive committee.

Risk workshops can be a very effective way of assessing the risks, and are often led by outside practitioners.

The sources of risk can be both internal and external. Some examples under each category are set out in Figure 5.5 on the next page.

The probability of an event happening and the impact that it would have on the business jointly determine how a risk is "ranked". Assessment of the latter needs to take into account any consequential loss not covered by insurance.

There can be a "domino effect" to adverse events. This can be seen in the crisis that hit Cadbury Schweppes in 2006. Following a salmonella scare, the company took the step of withdrawing more than a million confectionery products. The cost of the product recall was put at £5m but total losses were later estimated at £35m. The difference was reputational damage: customers lost confidence in the quality of the company's products and bought less chocolate.

FIGURE 5.5
EXTERNAL AND INTERNAL RISKS FOR A COMPANY

External risks

1. Inability to implement strategy due to lack of funds and low-rated share price

2. Government macro economic policy reduces market size and affects margins

3. Change of government hurts business environment

4. Adverse exchange rate changes affect sterling earnings

5. Demographic changes reduce market opportunity

6. Change in the indirect tax regime has negative impact on company profitability

7. Regulation change adds to cost or risk

Internal risks

1. Insufficient skilled people available to deliver the strategy

2. Impact of serious health and safety breaches

3. Reputational damage through product failure or inappropriate actions in the business or community

4. Failure to innovate to keep product or service offering relevant

5. Entry of new competitor with a significant cost advantage

6. Customer service failure due to IT or inadequate supply chain

7. Credit rating is downgraded; cost of borrowing materially increases

8. Executional failure of a large project due to inadequate project management

9. Loss of IT systems due to a disaster

10. Fraud or fraudulent accounting hits profits and affects reputation and market rating

11. Changes in assumptions increase the pension fund deficit

The domino effect also works in reverse: companies can be hit by something that happens to or action taken by one of their suppliers. Supply side risks are likely to be highest where the supplier base is small and limited to a few strategic relationships. In these circumstances, supplier failure is likely to have a particularly heavy impact on the company and on its customers.

Companies need to know and understand the risk analysis and risk management plan of their critical suppliers.

Some risks can be covered or part-covered by insurance, but these need to be effectively managed, too – if competitive premiums and future insurance are to be available.

Embedding risk assessment in the organisation

Effective risk control goes beyond compliance. It is not "bolted on" as a superstructure: it is part of the everyday management of the business or organisation.

Even where the exercise to "tick the governance box" is diligently done and reviewed during the year it means little without the culture to support it.

How do you embed risk assessment and control in the organisation? Here are a few pointers.

☐ Risk assessment and control should be aligned with the strategy and championed by the leadership. The direction the company has chosen must be assessed for risk; each risk must be identified and graded. As the strands of the strategy develop, they will need to be assessed in the same way.

☐ The broader environment in which the company trades should be annually assessed; the risks that have grown should be identified; so should those that have receded. The result may be a new "pecking order" of risks.

☐ "Sensing mechanisms" for changes in the broader environment make risk management more effective; companies are more resilient if they can act on early warning signs of increases to risk profiles.

☐ The subject of risk should feature on the agenda of the management committee quarterly, enabling the management of the high level risks to be regularly reviewed and the impact of any newly discovered ones to be regularly assessed.

- ☐ Individual operating boards should follow the same risk management steps as the group board.

- ☐ The risks of capital projects should be routinely examined; project managers should be especially pragmatic about executional risk.

- ☐ The audit committee should be the champion of risk assessment and control.

Summary

The Combined Code prescribes three subsets of the main board – the audit, nomination and remuneration committees. The requirements of the Code are clear that the permanent members of these committees should be non-executive directors, with executives invited to attend when necessary. (In smaller companies, the work of these committees is often absorbed into the total programme for the board, with all members participating.)

Each committee works to terms of reference, and these should be clearly laid down and regularly reviewed.

The audit committee has a pivotal role in governance and in providing assurance to the board. Its work is inextricably linked to risk assessment and control and can help optimise the value of projects.

Non-executive directors need to give a substantial and increasing amount of time to the work of the key committees such as audit and remuneration. Organisations need to consider the fees paid to the chairmen of these important committees carefully.

building
effectiveness

CHAPTER 6

The world we live in

We live in an imperfect world – or at least in a world made imperfect by some of its inhabitants.

Many of the business leaders I speak to feel frustrated by today's environment and question whether they can derive the same degree of satisfaction from their roles.

Elements of society take great delight in exposing the feet of clay of worthy institutions or those leading them. Self-interested elements of the media thrive on the negative, or sensational stories that generate more heat than light.

The antipathy of the public and the press towards business often seems matched by that of the legislators, who thrust yet more rules and regulations on already overburdened organisations. (The Companies Act 2006, which consolidates preceding laws, is still the longest piece of legislation on the UK statute book.)

Yet in some ways business has been its own worst enemy. Through financial failure, malfeasance, or simply by being asleep on their watch, directors have let themselves and their shareholders and stakeholders down. The media did not make Robert Maxwell up. And they did not invent the fall of Enron, WorldCom and Tyco in America, Parmalat in Italy and HIH in Australia.

Strategic failures

In addition to the spectacular scandals that have hit the headlines over recent years are many more failures where significant shareholder value has been lost through flawed or poorly executed strategy. A Booz Allen study of 1,200 firms, each with a market capitalisation of $1bn or more, found that:

☐   more shareholder value has been wiped out by mis-management and poor strategy execution than by all the worldwide corporate scandals;

☐   at the 360 worst firms, 87 per cent of the lost value was due to "strategic mishaps";

☐   only 13 per cent of lost value was due to regulatory compliance failures.

Booz Allen concluded that **codes such as Sarbanes-Oxley are really no more than quality-control mechanisms**. They do nothing to protect strategic and executional elements of the business.

Sarbanes-Oxley in the US and the Combined Code in the UK have been put in place to give assurance to the public and to stakeholders and to improve transparency. The irony is that some companies are now so preoccupied with ticking boxes and minimising the risks of being sued that **focus on building value through the right strategy and right ethos has been lost.**

It seems to me that trying to repair damage from breaches in professional standards or failures of integrity through application of a code is a bit like repairing the broken hinges on the stable door when the horse is long gone!

Trust has been diminished. And it will take more than a box-ticking approach to governance to rebuild it.

Reasons for low trust

The effect of corporate scandals, such as those listed above, has been to give the whole of business a bad name. With every company that unravels, the public becomes a little more cynical, trusts a little less.

Trust has also been eroded by:

☐ executive greed – a number of top executives have, over the years, received rewards wildly disproportionate to the value they've created and to the pay increases that have been awarded to more junior staff;

☐ "spin" – the rejection of "straight talk", perceived to be prevalent among politicians, has arguably made the public more cynical about leaders in all walks of life;

☐ underinvestment in people – many organisations have failed to spend time on the HR practices that build trust and value.

This last factor is, in my view, particularly important and particularly relevant to our discussion here. It is linked to the recent and current preoccupation with compliance and codes; **in many organisations, the human resource function has receded into the background while compliance and audit have been pushed to the fore.**

In both America and the UK, there is strong evidence that the psychological contract between worker and employer has been broken.

Results from three separate surveys in the US, recorded by the management guru Stephen M R Covey, showed that:

☐ only 51 per cent of employees have trust and confidence in senior management;

☐ only 36 per cent of employees believe their leaders act with integrity and honesty;

☐ 76 per cent of employees observed illegal or unethical conduct at work over a 12-month period.

A British report by the Council for Excellence in Management and Leadership (CEML) is similarly depressing. In summary:

☐   only 11 per cent of leaders are deemed to be inspiring by their staff;

☐   one third of all managers and half of junior managers rate leadership in their organisation as poor – with the public sector recording the worst scores.

Building blocks of better performance

Organisations need to place high trust high on their agendas if they're to deliver value to their shareholders over the long term and make the greatest possible contribution to society.

All organisations will perform better if they're clear about their **vision, mission and values**. These are the building blocks of effectiveness.

Vision and mission statements are often criticised for being vague or for having limited value. Although they're ultimately only as effective as the strategy and action plans that support them, to dismiss them as imprecise is to fail to understand their motivational value.

Some companies will talk about their purpose rather than their vision; they will give a central, motivational reminder of why the organisation exists. Hewlett Packard, for example, see its purpose as to "be respected by our customers, our people and society".

Vision, mission and strategy are interdependent. **Without a clear idea of the destination, the strategy of the organisation has limited meaning.**

Values set out the behaviours expected of employees in an organisation. They are the style, the character and the philosophy of the organisation: its *ethos*. A clear idea of values is very important in organisations where decisions are delegated as close as possible to the point of impact.

Getting the *right people* in the *right role* through effective recruitment techniques will deliver results. But people need to be challenged if they're to find their work stimulating and rewarding (see Figure 6.6 below). Evidence suggests that one of the greatest motivators for the talent in an organisation is the ability to grow and develop, to use initiative and judgment within clearly defined boundaries. To make the right decisions, people will need to have as their frame of reference the values of the organisation.

Values are not vague notions held in the locker of good processes for the sake of political correctness. They are an invaluable aid to the right behaviour.

There is an increasing trend in the boardrooms of the western world to have sensing and monitoring systems that test whether values are in embedded in the organisation. (See chapter 1, under "testing the statement of values".)

Strategy must be communicated effectively, and clear, supportive objectives must be given to the staff. In the best organisations, appraisals are an essential part of the vision, mission and values mix.

Trust and value creation

When there is mutual trust between members of an organisation, things happen more quickly and more cost-effectively. When there is mutual trust and a clear focus and purpose, and an effective system for delivery, an organisation creates optimum value for its shareholders.

High levels of trust lead to high morale, which in turn makes it easier to recruit, motivate and retain the best people, which in turn improves performance. The "high-trust organisation" therefore develops **a virtuous circle of value**; it satisfies shareholders and stakeholders and the communities in which it operates.

Understanding trust

The most comprehensive approach to understanding trust is found in Stephen M R Covey's 2006 book, *The Speed of Trust*. Covey talks about the five waves of trust – the five levels or contexts in which we establish trust.

The first wave is **self trust** or confidence and the ability we have to demonstrate our own trustworthiness and to inspire trust in others.

The second is **relationship trust**, building and maintaining trust with others.

Third is **organisational trust** – how leaders can generate trust to make the organisation more cohesive and effective.

Fourth is **market trust** – the reputation of the individual or a brand or the organisation itself.

The fifth wave is **societal trust**, the value the organisation creates by making a broader contribution or giving back to society.

Covey's approach is a very useful reminder of the dimensions and far-reaching nature of trust.

Whichever dimension we concentrate on, we should be clear that we will be judged on our actions and not our words. Words are useful pointers to or a precursor of behaviour but their meaning must be embedded in our every action. Hypocrisy and inconsistency destroy trust.

It is easy to set down and publish our values in a booklet; more difficult to follow them in practice. An organisation's values must be reflected in decision-making at every level. I want to spend time in this chapter looking at the personal qualities individuals need to develop trust and be more effective in the workplace.

Trust and integrity

Warren Buffett has said he looked for three things when he hired people: personal integrity, intelligence and a high energy level. He emphasised the first as the most important.

Employers wishing to follow his advice should note that you do not have to rely on the CV or resumé or on your subjective judgment during the interview. There are objective measures that can give greater certainty of a candidate's suitability and highlight the areas where more information will be needed. Good pyschometric tests have been developed for integrity, where consistency of responses can be verified.

A useful starting point is to understand what the word **integrity** means. The literal definition is helpful: integrity is a state of completeness, wholeness and *unbrokenness*. It is about **deeply held principles and beliefs**. It is not a rules-based model, and it cannot be captured in the depths of corporate manuals or governance procedures. It is about having a personal code and a set of values that don't break or *disintegrate* under pressure.

We need to demonstrate integrity because if we don't, reputation, our most valuable resource, is weak. Integrity is not about words and lofty ideals. It is about our actions and the *pattern of consistency* that we can find in them. It is the opposite of duplicity; it is about being open and transparent.

Integrity, in other words, is synonymous with trustworthiness.

Trust is at its highest when there is a spirit of openness and where challenge is invited. Integrity and hubris do not go together; leaders should have no difficulty in sharing goals and the progress towards them, in listening to and accepting, where appropriate, input from all levels. In this environment, the team will implement agreed actions effectively, efficiently and enthusiastically.

Skills and self-awareness

To build trust and confidence among followers and their peer group, a person needs not only integrity but also competence. This makes an objective assessment of the **skills set** of the individual against the requirements of the job essential.

In the best organisations, the competencies of each individual are reviewed against the needs of their role annually, and development plans are drawn up and implemented to address any shortfalls.

In my experience, the employee who undertakes a personal review, ahead of development discussions, has the advantage. The personal review must, however, be pragmatic; early on in a career, it can tend to revert to wishful thinking.

The analysis will need to review the technical skills required now and for future promotion, broader competencies such as strategic knowledge, communication skills, ability to influence, track record of delivery, and personality. A simple self-assessment checklist is set out in Figure 6.1.

To build trust at the personal level, we need to know ourselves and be prepared to develop the areas where improvement is needed. **Learning is continuous, no matter what level we have reached in an organisation.**

Trust requires knowledge and performance that earn the respect and confidence of those we work with and those who follow us. In the armed forces, the ranks are instilled with the need to trust their officers and, in return, officers need to demonstrate that that trust is well-placed.

It is helpful to have a tool that enables us to look at competencies in a consistent, objective manner. Thinking from a prospective employer's view is not a bad approach.

Figure 6.2 is a competency-based interview rating form for the position of marketing manager. Here, the job requirements were judged by the employer to be:

- ☐ strategic thinking;
- ☐ creativity;
- ☐ knowledge of market research methods;
- ☐ analytical orientation;
- ☐ oral communication skills;
- ☐ the ability to influence.

FIGURE 6.1
SELF-AWARENESS CHECKLIST

1. What is my preferred style of working?

   What are the positive aspects of this?

   What are the negatives?

   What actions do I need to take?

2. How much do I really know about:

   ☐ the industry (or wider voluntary sector in the case of a charity);

   ☐ the organisation;

   ☐ the products;

   ☐ technology and processes;

   ☐ customers;

   ☐ competitors;

   ☐ the drivers of value?

3. What is my level of understanding of external factors that affect my current role? Am I curious? Do I search out new trends that might have an impact on my role?

4. How deep and how extensive is my professional knowledge?

   Have I kept up to date?

   How do I rate against my peers inside and outside the current employer?

5. What progress have I made in personal learning and development over the past 12 months? (Give specific examples.)

6. How are my relations with:

   ☐ superiors;

   ☐ subordinates;

   ☐ peers;

   ☐ networks?

   Do I work well as a team member?

   Have I authenticated these views through 360 degree feedback?

FIGURE 6.2
COMPETENCY-BASED INTERVIEW RATING FORM

Candidate _____ Date _____

Interviewer _____ **Position** Marketing manager

Criteria	Evidence	Rating
Organising/planning		
Strategic thinking		
Creativity		
Knowledge of market		
research methods		
Analytical orientation		
Oral communication skill		
Other information		

Scale: 5 Well above; 4 A little above; 3 Meets the standard requirement; 2 A little below; 1 Well below.

The individual can think of their current job description, their current roles and "duties", and provide the evidence that they would give in an interview situation. Objectivity is the key: the self-assessment should be informed by 360 degree feedback.

Correcting bad habits

Why do some people stay stuck at the same level in an organisation and others reach the top? In his book, *What Got You Here Won't Get You There*, Marshall Goldsmith says the difference is not skill or intelligence but *behaviour*. There comes a point, he says, when bad habits hold you back.

This means that you need to do all you can to correct (or ameliorate) bad habits as early as you can. The first step will be to identify the negative traits – those that are part of your personality and those that may have crept in over time. A self-awareness checklist (see Figure 6.1) will help; so, too, will a good appraisal process and 360 degree feedback. (Your spouse or partner may also provide useful insights!)

Don't, warns Goldsmith, make the mistake of thinking that the way you've behaved in the past will be good enough to get you to where you want to be in the future. So what are the fatal behavioural flaws? Goldsmith highlights 20 bad habits, and I briefly summarise these at Figure 6.3

FIGURE 6.3
BAD HABITS THAT HOLD YOU BACK

- [ ] Hyper competitiveness
- [ ] Modifying the perfectly acceptable decisions of others
- [ ] Asking colleagues for ideas or opinions and then passing judgment on them
- [ ] Making destructive or caustic comments
- [ ] Starting a response with "no", "but" or "however" – all of which will stifle debate
- [ ] Letting all those around you know just how clever you are
- [ ] Speaking when angry *(I would also add "or when jet-lagged")*
- [ ] Negativity: "This won't work because ..."
- [ ] Withholding information
- [ ] Failing to give recognition and to praise
- [ ] Claiming credit you don't deserve
- [ ] Making excuses
- [ ] Clinging to the past: "The way we do things around here has always been ..."
- [ ] Making favourites of certain people and, perhaps, certain initiatives
- [ ] Refusing to say sorry *(Apologies should be face-to-face whenever possible)*
- [ ] Not listening
- [ ] Failure to express gratitude
- [ ] Punishing the messenger
- [ ] Passing the buck
- [ ] Being tolerant of your own shortcomings but intolerant of the shortcomings of others

---

Source: *What Got You Here Won't Get You There*, Marshall Goldsmith, Hyperion, 2007

Teams

Organisations value teamwork and the ability of individuals to work well together. Team-playing does not stifle creativity or the entrepreneurial spirit; it enhances them.

The effective team is made up of a rich combination of experiences and personality types and, often, diverse backgrounds. More than this, its collective talents are harnessed towards clear, common goals. Katzenbach and Smith, in their book *The Wisdom of Teams*, see the basic prerequisites as skills, accountability and commitment. Effective teams, they say, are performance-driven and offer significant opportunities for personal growth. One of their most important conclusions is that "teams strengthen the performance capability of the individuals".

Understanding how the individual personality types work and their preferred styles of working is essential for team members. There are a number of tools to help with this but, in my experience, one of the best is the Belbin Team roles. Figure 6.4 provides a brief summary of these and the "allowable weaknesses" in those who play them.

Communication and influencing skills

The ability to communicate is a core competence for managers today, whatever their role in the business or organisation. Motivating teams, controlling important projects, reinforcing strategy and values, and implementing part of a change programme, all require excellence in communication.

Excellence in communication brings with it greater self confidence. It therefore improves results. Through the virtuous circle of confidence, self-belief, more experimentation, greater success and, in turn, greater confidence, performance is improved.

The ability to communicate is one of the key aspects of personal influencing skills (see Figure 6.5).

Directors' attributes

As we've seen in earlier chapters, there must be a balance of skills and experience on the board that reflects the needs of the organisation. There is great benefit in understanding individuals' preferred styles of working, in understanding the dynamics of teams, in communicating well and creating the power to influence effectively.

FIGURE 6.4
BELBIN TEAM ROLES

Roles and Descriptions

Team Role Contribution	Allowable Weaknesses
Plant: Creative, imaginative, unorthodox. Solves difficult problems	Weak in communicating with and managing ordinary people
Resource Investigator: Extrovert, enthusiastic, communicative. Explores opportunities. Develops contacts	Loses interest once initial enthusiasm has passed
Co-ordinator: Mature, confident and trusting. A good chairman. Clarifies goals, promotes decision-making	Not necessarily the most clever or creative person in the group
Shaper: Dynamic, outgoing, highly strung. Challenges, pressurises and finds ways around obstacles	Prone to provocation and short-lived outbursts of temper
Monitor Evaluator: Sober, strategic and discerning. Sees all the options. Judges accurately	Lacks drive, speed and the ability to inspire others
Teamworker: Social, mild, perceptive and accommodating. Listens, builds, averts friction	Indecisive in crunch situations
Implementer: Disciplined, reliable, conservative and efficient. Turns ideas into practical actions	Somewhat inflexible; slow to respond to new possibilities
Completer Finisher: Painstaking, conscientious, anxious. Searches out errors and omissions. Delivers on time	Inclined to worry unduly. Reluctant to delegate
Specialist: Single-minded, self-starting, dedicated. Provides knowledge or technical skills in rare supply	Contributes only on a narrow front

One of the paradoxes of directorship is that it requires both independence of mind and the ability to collaborate with others to arrive at the right decisions. The wealth of experience and different backgrounds of the directors are brought together and *applied* to an issue before the board. (Effective boards avoid stultifying "group think" but that doesn't mean their members work in a vacuum.)

The Institute of Directors has identified several qualities and skills that are important for the board, irrespective of the type of the organisation. The IoD publication *Standards for the Board*, last revised in July 2006, lists a research-based set of personal attributes. The importance of each one will, of course, vary by organisation, but *Standards for the Board* says that "each of those deemed necessary by a particular board should be possessed by at least one director".

The attributes can be found among chairmen, managing directors, executive directors and non-executive directors. The list is long and should be read as a template for the **balanced board** rather than the skills set of any individual member.

FIGURE 6.5
KEY AREAS FOR PERSONAL INFLUENCING SKILLS

Area	Description
Knowledge	Technical knowledge, appropriate to the role
	Organisational knowledge
	Knowledge of industry or sector competitors, customers, suppliers
Communication style	Uses facts and figures to persuade
	Technically competent in relevant forms of communication
	Listens, evaluates and then responds
Awareness	Curious and alert to new trends that might have application
	Visible in the organisation
Attitude and approach	Avoids the use of hierarchical power; breaks down barriers across layers, teams and functions
Appearance and manner	Appropriate to the occasion

FIGURE 6.6
DIRECTORS' ATTRIBUTES

Strategic perception

Change orientation
Alert and responsive to the need for change. Encourages new initiatives and the implementation of new policies, structures and practices.

Creativity
Generates and recognises imaginative solutions and innovations.

Foresight
Is able to imagine possible future states and characteristics of the company in a future environment.

Organisational awareness
Is aware of the organisation's strengths and weaknesses and of the likely impact of decisions on them.

Perspective
Rises above the immediate problem or situation and sees the wider issue and implications. Is able to relate disparate facts and see all relevant relationships.

Strategic awareness
Is aware of the various factors that determine the company's opportunities and threats (for example, shareholder, stakeholder, market, technological, environmental and regulatory factors).

Decision-making

Critical faculty
Probes the facts, challenges assumptions, identifies advantages and disadvantages of proposals, provides counter arguments, ensures discussions are pertinent.

Decisiveness
Shows a readiness to take decisions and take action in the timeframe needed.

Judgment
Makes sensible decisions or recommendations by weighing evidence; considers reasonable assumptions, the ethical dimension and factual information.

Analysis and the use of information

Consciousness of detail
Insists that sufficiently detailed and reliable information, appropriate to the decision being taken, is considered, evaluated and tabled.

Eclecticism
Systematically seeks out all relevant information appropriate to the decision from a variety of sources.

Numeracy
Assimilates numerical and statistical information accurately; understands its derivation and makes sound interpretations.

Problem recognition
Identifies problems and possible or actual causes.

Communication

Listening skills
Listens dispassionately, intently and carefully so that key points are recalled and taken to account, questioning where necessary to ensure full comprehension.

Openness
Is frank and open when communicating; is willing to admit errors and shortcomings; is willing to take on board the views of others.

Verbal fluency
Speaks clearly, audibly and has good diction. Concise, avoids jargon; pitches the content to the audience's needs.

Presentation skills
Conveys ideas and images with clarity, with words appropriate to the audience and in a

memorable way.

Written communication skills

Conveys ideas, information and opinions accurately, clearly and concisely; writes intelligibly.

Responsiveness

Is able to invite and accept feedback.

Interaction with others

Confidence

Is aware of personal strengths and weaknesses. Is assured when dealing with others. Is able to take charge of a situation when appropriate.

Co-ordination skills

Adopts appropriate interpersonal styles and methods in guiding the board towards task accomplishment. Fosters co-operation and teamwork.

Flexibility

Adopts a flexible (but not compliant) style when interacting with others; takes their views into account and modifies a position when appropriate.

Presence

Has a strong, positive presence on first meeting; has authority and credibility; establishes rapport quickly.

Integrity

Is truthful and trustworthy and can be relied upon to keep his/her word. Does not have double standards and does not compromise on values, on ethical and legal matters.

Learning ability

Seeks and acquires new knowledge and skills from multiple sources, including board experience.

Motivation

Inspires others to achieve goals by ensuring a clear understanding of what needs to be achieved and by showing commitment and enthusiasm, encouragement and support.

Persuasiveness

Persuades others to give their agreement and commitment; in face of conflict, uses personal influence to achieve consensus and/or agreement.

Sensitivity

Shows an understanding of the needs and feelings of others, and a willingness to provide personal support or to take other actions as appropriate.

Achievement of results

Business acumen

Has the ability to identify opportunities to increase the company's business advantage.

Delegation skills

Distinguishes between what should be done by others and by him/her. Allocates decision-making or tasks to appropriate colleagues or subordinates and monitors their progress.

Exemplar

Sets challenging but achievable goals and standards of performance for self and others.

Drive

Shows energy, vitality and commitment.

Resilience

Maintains composure and effectiveness in the face of adversity, setbacks, opposition or unfairness.

Risk acceptance

Is prepared to take action that involves calculated appropriate risk in order to achieve the desired benefit or advantage.

Tenacity

Stays with a position or plan of action until the desired objectives are achieved or require adaptation.

Standards for the Board divides the attributes into six groups:

- ☐   strategic perception;
- ☐   decision-making;
- ☐   analysis and use of information;
- ☐   communication;
- ☐   interaction with others;
- ☐   achievement of results.

A number of these are components of leadership, dealt with more fully in the next chapter. *Standards for the Board* breaks each one down into sub-categories – see Figure 6.6 on the previous two pages. It's important to remember that there are objective measures for the extent to which a director has the attributes identified here. The indicators include 360 degree feedback, pyschometric tests and information gleaned from development workshops or from competency-based appraisals.

Work-related stress

Work-related stress is a big issue for countries in the developed world. Estimates of its impact on economies are not easy to make. The cost of days not worked is easy to compute, but the opportunity cost of lower productivity is much more difficult. In the UK, the Health and Safety Executive (HSE) puts the number of days lost to work-related stress, depression or anxiety at 10.5 million a year. The annual cost, according to the HSE, exceeds £10bn.

The changing economic and commercial context in which people work is frequently reported and well understood. The emphasis on cost reduction, downsizing (or "right sizing" as it is now euphemistically called) and the impact of new technology and offshoring are all adding to the pressures.

For those making the key decisions, the stresses can be acute, particularly if accompanied by a sense of loneliness or isolation. There are occasions when so many issues seem to be pressing down on the director that it is far from easy to cope.

The effective director understands how to identify and deal with personal stress and the stress of others in the organisation.

Dealing with personal stress

Given the wonderful complexity of people and the different ways they react to stress, there is no magic or foolproof formula. Common sense and experience, however, suggest a general approach to managing stress. Some of the key elements of this are given below.

- ☐ Get a balance in life. Make time for family, friends and outside interests. Have a personal fitness regime and ensure you stay healthy.

- ☐ Understand your natural susceptibility to stress. People who are naturally analytical may be particularly stressed by deadlines and the unavailability of information.

- ☐ Prioritise. Understand the difference between urgent and important tasks.

- ☐ Delegate where possible and appropriate. Give space for the delegatee to perform but do not abdicate responsibility for the final task. Accept support from others.

- ☐ Have a mentor or trusted person to talk to.

- ☐ Make time at work for reflection, prioritisation and feedback from staff. "Diarise" thinking time; and treat it as a priority.

- ☐ Trust your judgment; once a decision is made, get on with implementation. Nothing is more debilitating that continually questioning past decisions; mistakes are learning experiences.

- ☐ Have a personal development programme to ensure new and improved skills, and make sure there's a process to keep you fully up-to-date on key areas.

Stress in the organisation

The chief executive of one large international company believed that the best way to discover the true talent in an organisation was to maintain what he called "creative tension" among his senior executives. He would deliberately have loosely described, overlapping objectives; he would put a task out and see who would pick it up and perform best: "I like to throw a bone on the floor and see which dog gets to it first".

The organisation did not perform well, there was a lot of friction, and those who rose to the top were all of a similar "dog eat dog" style. Clashes at the top were inevitable, as was sub-optimal performance.

Effective leaders understand that excessive, continuous stress in the organisation will not deliver the best results or retain the best talent.

While it is recognised that stress can have a positive effect in delivering a project to a pre-determined timetable, and that self-induced stress pushes a person to higher levels of attainment, the evidence is that prolonged stress is unhelpful and that deep-seated stress in an organisation will adversely affect performance.

Directors need to be aware of the things that have the potential to create the kind of stress that will damage the business and the organisation and increase costs. Prevention is better than cure.

There is much to commend ongoing monitoring of the work environment in staff surveys. Some of the topics to be covered may include:

- management style and credibility;
- people's understanding of their roles and what is expected of them;
- pressures of work;
- the effect of change and uncertainty;
- the potential of the business, the industry or sector;
- the impact of strategy on work prospects;
- the potential of people to influence management and the ability to discuss personal issues;
- opportunities for self-development;
- pay and conditions;
- conflicts between personal values and perceived organisational values;
- personal issues; a person's own well being and health.

Indicators of stress

SHL Group, the occupational psychology specialist, has identified certain key indicators of work-related stress. The high-probability factors are listed in Figure 6.7.

An individual's ability to cope will, says SHL, depend partly on their personality. Indeed, the company has built a model that is an accurate predictor of stress by personality type.

FIGURE 6.7
HIGH-PROBABILITY INDICATORS OF STRESS

Highest Level 1	Lack of power
	Lack of clear objectives
	Teamwork and peer-group pressures
	Repetitive, routine work
Level 2	Lack of autonomy
	Poor promotional prospects
	Thwarted ambition
	No creative opportunity
	Severe time constraints; always under pressure
Level 3	Bureaucratic structures
Level 4	Lack of status
	Complex problem solving
Lowest Level 5	Dealing with the public
	Lack of consultation
	Few intellectual demands

One of the keys to stress control is to identify the root cause for each *individual*. Figure 6.7 represents the norms found by SHL research; they will vary in importance from person to person.

It is interesting for directors to note that "change and uncertainty", "delivering bad news", or "making tough decisions" scored lower than those triggers included in Figure 6.7.

Summary

Building effectiveness is not just about getting the basic competencies the organisation needs. It is about developing a high level of trust between members of the board – and, crucially, between them and all shareholders and stakeholders.

Trust takes time to build but is easily lost. Trust implies consistent behaviour, to standards set by the organisation and by the individuals within it.

In today's sceptical world, directors have a continuing role to show not only that they act in the best interests of their organisations but also that they pay due regard to employees, customers, suppliers and the wider communities in which they operate.

Sarbanes-Oxley or the Combined Code are really only quality-control checks; compliance with them is not proof of effectiveness.

There are good building blocks to better performance, and these include having a clarity of purpose and embedding values at every level of the organisation. Individual directors will wish to continually improve their skills and knowledge, and the first step is to truly understand themselves. The self-awareness check in this chapter is a useful starting point.

It is also helpful to pay attention to the team members' preferred methods of working; understanding the diversity on the board will improve its collective performance.

Getting the right people in the right roles requires a rigorous approach to selection; the existing skills sets on the board must be thought about carefully. Figure 6.6 lists desired director attributes. An organisation can use this as a template for the composition of its own board, deciding which attributes are essential for its particular needs and circumstances.

Prolonged and deep-seated stress – for example, that resulting from poor management of people – is the enemy of effectiveness. Directors need to be able to identify the root causes of stress for both themselves and the organisation and take steps to ameliorate them.

leadership

CHAPTER 7

Introduction

Leadership seems to be one of those things that are easy to spot but difficult to describe. You know it when you see it; but what exactly is it?

Many people start the search for definition by thinking of the difference between management and leadership. Managers focus on tasks such as planning, organising, staffing, directing and controlling; they are often "back stage". Leaders influence others and inspire people to follow them; they are clearly visible in the organisation.

But this distinction is of limited help. What does influencing others and inspiring people actually *mean*? What are the *practical components* of effective leadership?

As search consultants will affirm, there is a wide array of leaders across the diverse organisations serving the world's communities. They have different styles and, in many cases, different skills sets. But they share the same fundamental ingredients of leadership. Ian Odgers of the international executive search firm, Odgers Ray and Berndtson, sees these as:

- [ ] a vision that drives strategy and shapes the future;
- [ ] a pragmatism that translates the vision into strategic objectives;
- [ ] the ability to assess a situation accurately and absorb information quickly;
- [ ] the ability to set priorities that are aligned and focused, and implemented decisively.

Finally, he observes that "the best practitioners have a sound analytical ability matched by creativity and inventiveness".

Understanding and demonstrating leadership is of critical importance for the effective director but the same fundamental principles apply at all levels of management in all organisations.

Approaches to effective leadership

There are two distinct but related approaches to effective leadership. The first is to observe the behaviour of leaders, so that we can identify and promote those actions that are seen as value-adding, that will, if widely implemented, help get the best from the talent in the organisation. The second is to examine the underlying attributes of leaders in order to improve the identification, selection and development of leaders for the future.

The ability to lead is essential for those who are, or aspire to be, effective in management roles. It is also at the top of the list for organisations looking for promotable talent or for top executives.

Leadership behaviours

There are five main behavioural components of leadership; these are summarised in Figure 7.1.

FIGURE 7.1
FIVE DIMENSIONS OF LEADERSHIP

- ☐ Define the vision
- ☐ Commit to success
- ☐ Communicate freely, share goals, insights and approaches
- ☐ Challenge the status quo
- ☐ Develop personal characteristics of leadership (learn the skills)

Defining the vision gives the team a common goal. The leaders' passion for this goal must be seen in their actions as well as good motivating words: their support and belief in it must be unequivocal.

The second requirement of leadership is **commitment to success**. The leader will typically need to demonstrate energy, drive and the will to win. Effective leadership, however, is not about blind ambition: it requires the building blocks of success to be identified and monitored. As a New Zealand rugby coach said to his team, "the will to win is important but the will to practise and perfect is essential".

Third is the need to **communicate openly and share goals**, adjustments to them and the progress being made. When leaders see the need to depart from the prescribed course but fail to communicate the new direction to the troops, performance is sub-optimal. In extreme cases, the troops have been left marching to old orders, lemming-like to the cliff top, while the leader has found a better pathway down.

Fourth is **challenging the status quo**. The secret here is to have a culture where challenge is welcomed and invited and where new, more productive pathways are sought. The best leaders are capable of thinking the unthinkable and championing innovations that are aligned to the strategy whether they originated with them or not. They never dismiss ideas purely on the grounds that they weren't "invented here"; they don't demotivate young managers and graduates by saying "we don't do things that way here".

The **personal characteristics of leadership** include curiosity and thirst for knowledge; effective leaders draw on networks of information inside and outside the organisation and are widely read. The other key attributes are discussed in detail below.

Behavioural characteristics; attributes

A number of writers have, from their research, listed leadership attributes or behavioural characteristics that promote understanding of effective leadership.

Bill Mabey and I have identified specific behavioural characteristics frequently found among successful leaders. These are summarised in Figure 7.2

FIGURE 7.2
BEHAVIOURAL CHARACTERISTICS OF SUCCESSFUL LEADERS

- ☐ Ability to inspire others
- ☐ Enthusiasm
- ☐ Flexibility
- ☐ High intellect, and the ability to grapple with complex issues
- ☐ Ability to build relationships
- ☐ Trustworthiness; integrity
- ☐ Ability to communicate; ability to influence
- ☐ Ability to delegate
- ☐ Willingness to experiment
- ☐ Frankness

This can be compared with Figure 7.3, Howard Gardner's list, based on observations of American leaders.

FIGURE 7.3
GARDNER'S LEADERSHIP ATTRIBUTES

After studying a large number of North American organisations and leaders, Howard Gardner concluded that the person capable of leading in one situation could probably lead in another. He identified common threads connecting effective leaders. Some of the main ones are listed here.

- ☐ Physical vitality and stamina
- ☐ Intelligence and action-oriented judgment
- ☐ Eagerness to accept responsibility
- ☐ Task competence
- ☐ Understanding of followers and their needs
- ☐ Skill in dealing with people
- ☐ Need for achievement
- ☐ Capacity to motivate people
- ☐ Courage and resolution
- ☐ Trustworthiness
- ☐ Decisiveness
- ☐ Self-confidence
- ☐ Assertiveness
- ☐ Adaptability/flexibility

Sources of authority; types of leaders

The licence to lead is sometimes found in the power of the position the individual holds. This is particularly true in organisations that are naturally hierarchical. The military is, perhaps, the most obvious example, and some of the earliest references to leaders and their actions are rooted in a war theatre.

Leadership can also be emergent: the person "bubbles to the top" or emerges with the consensus of the group.

The mandate of the leader is a significant determinant of their effectiveness.

I like the description of the types of leaders proposed in R A Dale's 2002 translation of the *Tao Te Ching*:

"There are four types of leaders. The best is indistinguishable from the will of those that selected her.

The next best enjoys the love and praise of the people.

The poor leader rules through anarchy and fear, and the worst leader is a tyrant despised by the multitudes who are victims of his power.

What a world of difference between these leaders.

In the last two types, what is done is without sincerity or trust.

In the second type, there is harmony between the leaders and the people.

In the first type, whatever is done happens so naturally that no-one presumes to take the credit."

Robert Townsend, co-author of management book *Up the Organisation*, observed that "true leadership must be for the benefit of the followers, not the enrichment of the leader". While we may not agree 100 per cent with this concept, preferring to see leadership as being for the benefit of the organisation, there's much wisdom in the idea that followers must be the focus and that the leader must not be motivated by self-interest.

Followers

Leadership, as the above quote from the *Tao Te Ching* implies, is more effective when those who follow have a clear sense of direction and are loyal and committed to the cause. Loyalty cannot be commanded; it must be earned and constantly reinforced by continuous bond-building between the leader and follower. Kouzes and Posner recognised this in their study of more than 15,000 people from around the world. They found that the 10 words most used by followers to describe a good leader were:

- ☐ valued;
- ☐ motivated;
- ☐ enthusiastic;
- ☐ challenged;
- ☐ inspired;
- ☐ capable;

- ☐ supported;

- ☐ powerful;

- ☐ respected;

- ☐ proud.

High-level performance requires followers who are involved and informed. In order to maintain the high level of motivation that is characteristic of a well-led organisation, the thinking leader is constantly helping the constituents to improve their skills base and to develop as individuals. **Personal development is one of the most important motivators of employees in all organisations.**

Inspirational and perspirational leadership

Are leaders born or made?

The ability to inspire is often seen as linked to personal charisma. Minds are drawn to charismatic or high-profile people who have achieved prominence in their chosen fields. Charismatic leadership is often synonymous with heroic leadership, where the emphasis is very much on the individual and their achievements, rather than those of the team.

Experience has shown, however, that leadership skills can be learned, improved and mastered, provided there is the time and the resource devoted to this. You do not have to be a born charismatic to lead an organisation well.

And "star quality" does not guarantee success; leadership, as will be clear from other chapters, has to be worked at. Effectiveness depends on **both inspirational and perspirational leadership.**

Inspirational leadership

Key features of this are given below.

- ☐ The leader is very visible. They take every opportunity to see people in their own workplaces and use these opportunities to reinforce values and culture, and clarify objectives.

- ☐ The leader is the role model and "symbol" for other leaders in the organisation and is transparent in decision-making.

- ☐   The leader is the living ethical standard, aware that their actions are always under scrutiny, aware that actions validate the fine motivational words.

- ☐   The leader is *agent provocateur*, the non-conformist, the challenger of the status quo and agent for change.

- ☐   The leader has apostles who are energised and committed to the same cause; they rely on feedback that is direct and unbiased.

- ☐   The leader recognises the importance of excellent internal and external communications designed for the specific audience.

- ☐   The leader fights bureaucracy but does not destroy essential control.

Perspirational leadership

Perspirational leadership makes sure the energy and enthusiasm created by the inspirational leader are properly *channelled*. Without it, there will be a highly charged, motivated organisation that is directionless, that lacks the ability to deliver.

Perspirational leadership, in other words, is about *action*; the practical steps that are necessary to realise the vision.

The tools needed for delivery will include:

- ☐   a vision, mission and set of values that have been clearly communicated throughout the organisation;

- ☐   clarity of objectives that cascades down;

- ☐   organisational clarity that enables delivery;

- ☐   reward systems that are aligned with goals;

- ☐   compatibility of resource allocation and clarity of priorities;

- ☐   reporting mechanisms and controls that will enable the organisation to be measured correctly against suitable and pre-determined goals.

Successful leadership in practice

Great leaders have not only the power to inspire but also the ability to link their vision to the practical, more mundane tools of achievement. Leaders don't just lead; they also need to manage. This is the point that Ian Odgers makes in the earlier quote.

The leader achieves success through team-building, inculcating a spirit of openness and seeking out feedback from followers. They are committed to effective communication both inside and outside the organisation; **successful international top-level managers spend between 20 per cent and 25 per cent of their time communicating with internal and external stakeholders.**

The leader knows the power of continuous learning and the importance of refreshing their personal skills. They demonstrate this by placing a high priority on self-improvement and ensuring that management development is a key objective for all leaders in the organisation.

The particular style of leadership will, however, reflect the individual's own aptitudes and strengths. Leadership does not require re-invention: the leader does not have to become some "ideal" new personality, unrecognisable to those they lead; they can remain true to themselves. (Transformation or re-invention could, indeed, suggest a lack of personal integrity.)

Newly appointed directors

Thankfully, newly appointed directors today will in almost all cases have an induction programme. Where there is an agreed need, this will include special elements tailored to the individual and their role.

Executive directors are likely to have strong knowledge of the company and its operations; a non-executive director will need to develop this over time, starting during the induction phase.

An understanding of the memorandum and articles of association, and of the rights, duties and obligations of directors, is essential.

In addition, the new member will need to familiarise themselves with current issues for the board. Agendas and minutes for meetings over the previous 12 months, and discussions with the chairman and the secretary, will help them to understand the "live" and important issues for the organisation.

For listed companies, another good source of information is the broker's notes and those of competing analysts.

Discussions with the advisers, especially the auditor, are also advisable.

A development plan should emerge and be agreed with the chairman, reflecting individual needs.

In Figure 7.4 there is a suggested checklist for new directors.

FIGURE 7.4
NEW DIRECTOR'S CHECKLIST

☐ Am I clear about the legal requirements of the role of a director? In particular, do I have a good knowledge of the duties and liabilities of directors?

☐ Have I read and understood the powers in the memorandum and articles of association?

☐ Am I clear about the company's strategy and how it will be delivered?

☐ Have I received and understood the vision, mission and values of the company?

☐ Have I reviewed the agenda and minutes over the past 12 months; am I satisfied that the right items are discussed and covered at the board?

☐ Have I drawn up a schedule of visits or meetings, where needed, to improve my knowledge?

☐ Have I made the time to talk to key advisers and, where appropriate, some of the key shareholders?

☐ Is the information provided to directors concise and valuable; does it present a balanced view of the health and progress of the business against pre-determined goals?

☐ Are the minutes informative, listing areas for future action by individuals, and issued quickly after each meeting?

☐ Are the minutes of the main sub-committees of the board available to the directors?

At their first board meeting, the new director will spend most of their time observing and learning, contributing special knowledge as needed. Where appropriate, the sensitive chairman will take time briefing a new director on the context for significant items, or provide background information at the meeting.

Given the time constraints of the meeting, however, the wise new director will make a note of any areas they need more information on and follow them up later.

The meeting is a golden opportunity to observe the style and chemistry of the board.

Networking is an important element and this, together with informal discussion, often takes place over a lunch after the board meeting, or, increasingly, in a pre-board dinner the night before.

Summary

Much has been written about leadership by business book authors and consultants. However, it's important to stress that leadership is not an abstract or theoretical concept to be analysed and reduced to a formula. It cannot be packaged into capsules or "taken daily"; it is a living and inherent part of the director's role.

This chapter has not aimed to capture the concept by refined definition, but to talk about the relevant aspects of leadership as directors go about their business lives.

There is great merit in thinking about how followers feel about leadership and what words they would use to describe a "good leader". These point to the attributes and characteristics of effective leadership, listed in Figures 7.2 and 7.3.

There must be both "inspirational" leadership and "perspirational" leadership if the organisation is to succeed.

New directors or those who aspire to being a director must be equipped with the practical tools for leadership. These include knowledge, understanding and information.

people advantage

CHAPTER 8

Introduction

Talent has the potential to create value and improve collective performance. A key responsibility of directors is to ensure that the powerful force of people is released for the benefit of the organisation.

From our work for the book *The People Advantage*, Bill Mabey and I were clear that "putting the right people in the right jobs and encouraging the right development will enhance organisational efficiency, productivity and, where appropriate, profitability".

Two of the most important elements of a successful company (and this is also true for charities and NPOs) are the right strategy and the right people. In other words, **right strategy + right people = outperformance**.

"People are our most important asset" has become a mantra of leaders. In many organisations, however, it remains unsupported by the building blocks to manage people effectively. That's why I'm including this chapter in this book.

Directors must have a clear view of the processes behind the selection, motivation and development of their people; and they must make sure that the organisation will not be left vulnerable when top talent goes, that succession plans are robust and include both planned promotion and emergency "cover".

Key areas for improving the people resource

Before setting out to improve the talent in an organisation, the director must understand how the recruitment process works. There is clear evidence that greater productivity and better performance start here.

Too often, the recruitment process is sloppy and over-reliant on subjective elements such as the interview and the CV. When a final decision has been made, references are taken from people nominated by the candidate. With this approach, only about one in three appointments is considered to be successful.

The cost of poor candidate selection is too high – for both the employer and the employee – to take these kinds of risks.

How do you make the selection process better? The starting point is to spend time and effort thinking clearly about the key elements of the role and how these may change over the next few years, and from them prepare a job description.

Once the profile of the *ideal* candidate is established, there is a better chance of selecting someone *suitable*. Objective competency-based tests and personality profiles for the final candidates will help identify the closest "matches". If the results of these are available before the final interview, the interviewer can do a more rigorous job, exploring any areas of inconsistency or asking for more information to substantiate the candidate's claims.

More rigour and time need to be put not only into the selection process but also into the development of people. When "successful managers" claim to spend less than four per cent of their time on personal development and training and devote only eight per cent of their time to development of the people resource, something has clearly gone wrong.

Non-executive directors are not expected to be HR experts, but they should be keenly interested in the selection and development of people and in making sure "human capital" is an issue for the board.

Figure 8.1 is a checklist of areas to focus on and principles to remember when improving HR performance.

Management development and succession planning

This is one of the most important items the directors will discuss. It should rank alongside the strategy session, risk assessment and controls, and the annual budget exercise. From feedback that I have received in recent years and from my own observations, however, it is not given the weighting it deserves.

Where a process for management development and succession planning exists (e.g. in larger companies) it tends to be inadequate and heavily biased towards *form*. **The importance of having a meaningful discussion at the board is often missed.**

Directors have a responsibility to understand the basis on which management potential is identified and followed up with individual development programmes.

They will also be keenly interested in the implications of the management review for succession planning. This is a top-level overview for the board that is usually undertaken annually, following on from the strategy discussions. It is built up from individual actions and appraisals but, crucially, is set in the context of the changing environment. Trends and implications are evaluated, as are opportunities and threats that are likely to have future impact. Directors will have some key questions.

FIGURE 8.1
KEY PRINCIPLES FOR PERFORMANCE IMPROVEMENT

Select the right people

The recruitment process should attract the most appropriate candidates

Job analysis is essential

The effectiveness of the recruitment process should be monitored

Recruiting internally (where possible) can motivate others and improve efficiency

Train and develop people in the right way

Raise expectations in recruits; give people the tools (support, training and experience) to achieve their personal best

Match skill development to the business needs for today and for tomorrow

Draw up personal development plans for each employee and make sure these are regularly reviewed and amended at appraisal time

Communicate effectively

The mission and strategy should be clearly stated and widely communicated

Values must be clear, comprehensible and practised

Key messages, including success stories, should be communicated through a structured programme

Individual and organisational performance should be clearly communicated

Make sure everyone is clear about their roles

Personal objectives should cascade down from corporate objectives and must be understood; performance evaluation against these should be objective and clear

Appraisals are for all – from the chairman to the staff members

Motivate employees at all levels

Employees must feel valued and empowered to act, and they must be competent in their roles

Reward systems must be aligned to the needs of the business and be competitive as well as motivating

Employee "ownership" (responsibility and initiative) is a good thing and should be encouraged

Create a spirit of curiosity in the organisation

Always be outward-looking

Encourage experimentation – there is always a better way

☐ Have the external trends been identified and evaluated in the strategy process; have the implications for skills been properly reflected?

☐ Looking at the strategy, have the implications for the quantity and quality of the people been correctly reflected?

☐ What are the steps being taken to identify the managers of significant potential?

☐ Are the right development opportunities being offered to managers with potential? Does their personal development plan take full account of the opportunities that are likely to be offered?

☐ Are the "peaked managers" (usually a high proportion, see Figure 8.2) being given opportunities to improve?

☐ How does the organisation propose to deal with the "blockages" – people who will impede progress and possibly destroy value?

☐ What are the succession issues both on a planned basis and on an emergency basis? (Special and individual attention must be paid to the roles at the top of the organisation and those that are one level beneath them.)

Model of executive potential

In many organisations, identifying the very top talent is far too subjective an exercise. Inconsistencies arise when different managers make assessments in different ways. Input from the human resource director can create a level playing field for all the people proposed; and having a common assessment template helps.

In smaller firms, perhaps where there is no human resource director, the managing director is likely to have a good, rounded view.

Assessment centres where young managers take pre-determined "tests" under observation are a good way of introducing more objectivity (see further under "assessing potential").

There are two important elements to consider: performance and potential. The former can be assessed through a high-quality appraisal process. The latter is best assessed through special assignments and multiple programmes that simulate work/management situations, the results of which are summarised in a form that can be understood by the board and allows comparisons to be made over time.

FIGURE 8.2
MODEL OF EXECUTIVE POTENTIAL

	High potential		
Low performance	Questionmarks	High flyers	High performance
	Blockages	Peaked managers	
	Low potential		

Set out in Figure 8.2 is the model of executive potential, which gives a good picture of the shape of the talent pool.

The key to understanding this is given below.

☐ **The high flyers** are the people of high performance and high potential. Here the imperative is to find roles that motivate them, give further insights into their potential and challenge their abilities in new areas. (This may involve some risk taking.) Typically, 15 per cent of the executive population would be here.

☐ **Question marks** are people who are not performing well in their current roles but have high potential. Often, the organisation will be failing them. There is a need to ask, "Are they in the right role? Are they sufficiently motivated or well managed?" Typically, 10 per cent of the total.

☐ **Peaked managers** make up the bulk of employees. They perform well but have little or no extra potential. Here the task is to add to their skills to improve their effectiveness in their current role or a role that is similar. They are the biggest group, typically 65-70 per cent of the total.

☐ **Blockages** are those of low potential and low performance. They need to be removed from their current role – and, probably, from the organisation. In a well-run organisation, they usually account for less than five per cent, but in others may be as high as 10 per cent.

Foundation for managing people more effectively

We have seen the importance of aligning the people plan with the strategy, so that the current and future needs of the business are met. Fundamental to this is clarity of corporate objectives and then clarity of the derived objectives and personal goals for employees. Aligned to these is the reward system, which should reinforce the importance of delivery.

FIGURE 8.3
KEY ELEMENTS OF AN APPRAISAL

Element	Description
1. Background	A brief description of the key factors that may have influenced performance for the period under review, paying special regard to external factors.
2. Comments on objectives	Identification of the key achievements in the review period and any goals not achieved or partially achieved.
3. Management development and team building	The part of the appraisal that underlines the absolute importance of the manager's priorities and discusses progress towards goals.
4. Comments on overall performance	This is the summary that encapsulates the overall performance and highlights any areas of weakness/disappointment.
5. Comments on style and job competencies	This part of the appraisal is made more objective by 360 degree feedback. Discussion should be two-way and should include interpersonal skills, qualities of leadership, time management and areas where additional or improved competencies are needed.
6. Training and development plans	After 5 above, development areas are identified and a plan agreed that will be followed up by the HR department. The training needs of all will be summarised for the board overview report.
7. Career aspirations	A full career review is best carried out at a separate time from the appraisal, but a brief discussion here is helpful. There should be an opportunity to talk about aspirations (and their validity), along with training needs and the competencies to be acquired or developed in the agreed timeframe.
8. Additional items	This allows time for any other relevant item.

It will, therefore, be readily seen that the foundation on which good management development and succession plans are built is the **appraisal system**.

The approach to appraisals will vary not only according to the needs of the organisation but also the position the person holds. For some people in an organisation, the competency-based appraisal is best. Here, the focus will be on the extent to which the individual has the key competencies for their job; a personal development plan will then evolve.

At higher management levels, the focus is commonly on achieving objectives and personal goals that may have bonus entitlement attached to them. I set out in Figure 8.3 on the previous page a suggested template for a simple but effective approach to this type of appraisal.

People not processes

For appraisals to be effective, they must be more than token, box-ticking exercises. If they degenerate into mere "data gathering", they will cause anger and frustration and do little to enhance the reputation of the human resources department.

Regrettably, some professional human resource directors and consultants focus more on the process than the results. In one company I've worked with, the instructions to managers for the appraisal process ran to more than 10 pages, with the emphasis on conformity: data had to be easily document-read into the computer. This was an unsuccessful model: people development should never be this impersonal.

My approach is to keep things simple but to avoid superficiality. Both the appraiser and the person being appraised should thoughtfully prepare for the discussion, after which the appraiser should prepare notes in the form of Figure 8.3. These will then be signed by both parties. Based on the grandfather principle, the appraisal will be reviewed and noted by the appraiser's boss, who will be invited to add comments.

The individual should be at the heart of the appraisal system. And there should be clear recognition that the process is two-way. The training and development of a member of an organisation is a dual responsibility. While the organisation has a real obligation, the initiative should be with the individual. **A person's development and career are too important to be left solely to the employer.**

Assessing potential

Directors will need to be satisfied that the spotting of talent is not left to chance and that no-one is being overlooked.

In smaller companies, it will be relatively easy to have a comprehensive view of the potential of individuals. The senior managers will know their work habits, observe their styles, and measure their ability to handle new tasks.

In much larger organisations, the task is trickier. The most basic approach is for top management to meet with the human resource director and discuss the names that each manager has put forward. Since each manager may be looking for different things, this has the disadvantage of being random and subjective. It can be given more rigour and be made more "scientific", however, by a sound appraisal system; the evidence of appraisals can be used to inform discussions.

Increasingly, given the vital importance of having the right people in the right roles, employers are using tools to make the approach more effective. These include 360 degree feedback exercises and psychometric tests that assess personality and the areas needed for the top. A more rigorous approach still can be found in assessment centres. These use psychometric tests and management simulation exercises that can be tailor-made to test the competencies that the employer sees as essential for future executive talent. They usually require an investment of a couple of days.

In Figure 8.4 is a list of desired competencies for managers capable of rising to board level within three years. It was set out by a FTSE 350 company.

FIGURE 8.4
COMPETENCIES FOR MANAGERS OF POTENTIAL

- [ ] Has the ability to think and act strategically; sees the big picture

- [ ] Inspires a shared vision, a common set of goals, and lives out the values in decision-making

- [ ] Has the ability to lead others, motivates individuals and teams to deliver agreed objectives

- [ ] Provides stability and direction

- [ ] Delegates tasks appropriately and effectively, leaving specifics to others

- [ ] Shows organisational awareness in decision-making

- [ ] A team person

Summary

Performance will always be sub-optimal if the talent in the organisation is under-developed and under-exploited.

"Human capital" should be a priority for the boardroom. Developing and motivating people should have equal "billing" with strategy creation and implementation.

As well as spending sufficient time on their own development, directors should spend sufficient time on the development of others.

Figure 8.1 suggests a checklist of areas to focus on to improve HR performance. There is a need for clear personal objectives that are aligned with the overall strategy and for a robust appraisal system.

The board will need to review the appraisal process and a summary of the results from it. The model of executive potential in Figure 8.2 can be used to create a snapshot of the talent at a particular time.

Because an organisation will depend upon the managers of potential for future leadership, Figure 8.4 gives an example of the competencies looked for by a FTSE 350 company.

small and medium-sized companies

CHAPTER 9

Introduction

Much of the content of this book applies to organisations of all sizes. Small and medium-sized enterprises (SMEs) are, however, worthy of a chapter in their own right.

SMEs are inevitably overshadowed in the public consciousness by the big, household-name businesses that hit the headlines. But they make a vital contribution to the economy. In 2001, they employed, according to Cabinet Office figures, 56 per cent of the UK workforce.

The shape of the SME sector

The DTI defines a small business as one employing fewer than 50 people and a medium-sized company as one employing between 51 and 250 people. Within these brackets is great diversity.

The SME sector spans very small owner-manager businesses with only a handful of employees, small but dynamic enterprises that have high-growth potential (e.g. biotech spin-outs), family-owned and family-operated businesses incorporated as limited liability companies, and growing but relatively mature companies that are closer to the larger public company model.

Nonetheless, members of the SME sector face common issues. This chapter discusses the key areas of consideration. It also examines the particular challenges faced by family businesses.

Legal duties of directors

All SMEs operate in the same legal and regulatory framework.

The rules governing directors (and their equivalents) have been examined in some detail in chapter 2. For the sake of context, some of the most important points are repeated here.

- ☐ A company is a **separate legal entity** from those who run it or put up the capital. It has both shareholders and stakeholders and *exists* in the communities where it operates. Directors owe it responsibilities.

- ☐ The legal obligations of directors apply whether they hold executive or non-executive roles.

- [ ] The company's constitution (memorandum and articles of association) comprises its *by-laws*. It will define what the company can and cannot do, specify the number of directors and how they can be appointed or removed, and set out the rights between shareholders. Changes to the constitution need shareholder approval.

- [ ] In the UK, the Companies Act 2006 sets down much of the legal framework for directors. It includes a code of director's duties, central to which is the principle that a director must act in a way that they consider most likely to **promote the success of the company for the benefit of its members as a whole.**

- [ ] Directors' duties and liabilities arise under common law as well as the Act, and from UK or EU regulations covering areas such as health and safety, the environment, employment and tax.

- [ ] A copy of the constitution must be available to the public at Companies House. In addition, directors of limited companies and limited liability partnerships must file annual returns and accounts with the registrar of companies. *There are penalties for late filing.*

- [ ] Companies must keep proper records, including minutes of meetings, books of account and financial statements. *The accounts must be audited if the profit exceeds £500,000.*

- [ ] Shadow directors, people who have a history of influencing the board's decision-making, can be subject to many of the same legal obligations as the formally appointed members. *(The chairman must make the status of those attending meetings clear in the minutes.)*

- [ ] Directors need to pay special attention if the company is at risk of becoming insolvent – i.e. of having insufficient assets to cover its liabilities or being unable to meet payments as they fall due. (This is comprehensively discussed in chapter 8 of the IoD's sister publication *The Director's Handbook*.)

Governance

SMEs (like all organisations operating today) are increasingly expected to go beyond their strict legal obligations. Good governance is not just about operating within the law; it is about observing best business practice.

The importance of good governance has been underlined in chapter 3. Worldwide, there is clear evidence of a high correlation between poorly performing companies and low levels of governance. Enron, Worldcom, Parmalat and HIH collapsed spectacularly after spectacular failures in governance.

The corollary is that companies with high standards of governance receive a higher rating from investors and from lenders.

But is there really a *business case* for smaller companies, which are usually less dependent on the good opinion of institutional investors and which have very different ownership structures from the big, public corporates, to pursue good governance?

The answer depends partly on what you understand by "good governance". If you think of it purely in terms of box-ticking and compliance, it's no. If, as I do, you see it as creating standards and behaviours that *add value*, it's an unequivocal yes.

The next question, therefore, has to be, **"Are SMEs as interested in governance as they should be?"**

I've been genuinely impressed by the number of directors of small businesses who want to do the right thing for their companies in terms of governance. In the 2005 IoD Scotland survey, 84 per cent of SME directors considered corporate governance as "essential to their company's prospects".

However, from the feedback I get, understanding of the principle that governance is good for business is not matched by an understanding of how and why.

Before we examine the role of governance in adding value, we need to know a bit more about how SME directors see the state of governance in their companies.

Governance: what SME directors think

Feedback from members of the IoD who are directors of SMEs makes it clear that they take their responsibilities seriously and try to ensure that standards of governance in their companies are at a level commensurate with their size and ownership. A special survey of 3,774 directors, from which 189 usable replies were received, revealed a high level of satisfaction with governance structures and control environments.

Among these SMEs:

☐   boards meet regularly, with 65 per cent meeting quarterly or more often, and agendas and board conduct are generally viewed as positive;

☐ the board is seen to have the right balance of skills and is not seen to be dominated by one individual;

☐ topics such as strategy, succession planning, risk assessment and control, the control environment, and health and safety are all seen to be an important part of the board agenda;

☐ audited accounts are prepared by 78 per cent of the sample, and are seen to provide value to stakeholders;

☐ communication channels with staff on the progress of the company exist in 91 per cent;

☐ 65 per cent think independent directors add real value.

While these results are very positive, they are no cause for complacency. They are but a snapshot of the state of governance in Britain's SMEs; they are not the full picture.

Respondents to surveys like these are naturally more likely to be positive in their approach to these issues. There will be many other companies that have much further to go. And, importantly, the results are not really a qualitative measure of governance. They don't tell us how the personal standards of the respondents compare with best governance practice. And they say little about the value good governance actually creates in their organisations.

Governance focus for SMEs

What should be the priorities for SMEs that want to improve performance through better governance? Given the diversity of the sector, there is no universal, "one size fits all" approach. However, I believe it's helpful to set out the key areas to address. Figure 9.1 is a governance checklist for SMEs.

In all of this, it is important to emphasise that the *essence* of the organisation (see vision, mission and values, page 131) is what matters. The detailed process can be relatively light. SMEs that associate governance with bureaucracy have missed the point. Good governance, as Figure 9.1 shows, essentially just means running your organisation well.

One of the key challenges is to demonstrate to stakeholders that you can be depended upon to maintain high standards and avoid nasty surprises. This makes a review of the accounts and the control environment of vital importance. In smaller companies, this is often carried out with the full board, including the executives. There is, though, a strong case for a concurrent review by an audit committee, led by an independent non-executive.

FIGURE 9.1
GOVERNANCE CHECKLIST FOR SMEs

The key questions

☐ Is there a division of duties on the board; is power shared? Is there "objective challenge" – either by a non-executive director/non-executives or, perhaps, a mentor?

☐ Is there an audit committee led by a financially literate non-executive director that can objectively review the accounts and the control environment?

☐ Have we appointed an auditor to give assurance to all stakeholders? If not, can we justify this?

☐ Does the board review the health and safety environment at least annually?

☐ Does the board understand its legal obligations? Is compliance monitored by directors?

The key processes

Compliance with the Combined Code, which many SMEs see as the gold standard of governance, does not, as chapter 6 made clear, provide assurance against failure. It will mean little without the **building blocks of good governance**. For the vast majority of SMEs, these will include:

☐ a strategic plan – a document that sets out the direction of the company, the milestones to be achieved and the resources and structures necessary for successful execution and delivery;

☐ risk assessment and control – a system to identify high-level risks and the steps to ameliorate them;

☐ a budget or annual operating plan for the strategy;

☐ a values statement that is communicated so clearly to staff that it informs every important decision made in the organisation;

☐ an annual succession and employee development plan – vital if the company is a fast-growing business or one where the owner-manager is planning their exit;

☐ a pragmatic appraisal process rooted in effective two-way communication;

☐ a management information system that provides regular relevant information on the progress and health of the business. (For some, this will mean monthly accounts and key performance indicators that move beyond financial measures; for others, it will mean quarterly reporting on the state of the business.)

Vision, mission and values

Studies of successful directors in small and medium-sized companies show that they have a clear idea of where they want their company to be in the future and a business plan to get there.

The best, most rigorous approach is to commit these ideas to writing. The business plan, essential for securing government grants or other funding, should include a *written statement* of the company's mission.

Further, there should be a clear vision for the organisation, communicated effectively and clearly to employees and other stakeholders, and a clear set of values. Again, these should be committed to writing.

In setting vision, mission and values, directors distil the essence of the business and communicate it clearly with the minimum of fuss and process. The model of distinguishing vision, mission and values discussed in chapters 1 and 3 is a useful way to get discipline here.

For owner-managers, the process of setting vision, mission and values, can, of course, be problematic. The goal of selling the business within a prescribed timeframe or handing it on to a family member may not be the most motivating for staff. The solution is to have a business-oriented mission and set of values that transcend any ownership changes.

The owner-manager will also want to discuss the ownership aim openly with other directors and key employees, making sure that there will be a process of consultation and that the future of the organisation's people will be an important consideration in any decision.

Information to manage the business

Owner-managers are usually much closer to the business and typically need less information, less regularly. This is especially true where there are no other significant shareholders or independent directors on the board. However, it is still desirable to review the regular information needed for managing the business.

Set out in Figure 9.2 is a list of questions that should help identify and decide the information needs of the business. For illustrative purposes, I've included hypothetical answers.

FIGURE 9.2

QUESTIONNAIRE TO ESTABLISH INFORMATION NEEDS OF THE BOARD

Question	Response
1. How often will the board meet?	Quarterly
2. What financial information is needed for these meetings?	P&L against budget and last year, balance sheet and cashflow Analysis of stock and debtors, forward order book
3. What non-financial information is needed?	An update on the trading environment and on productivity and human resources
4. What input do we need before we file statutory accounts?	Reports and statements from the auditor, who should attend the relevant board meeting(s) Review of the control environment
5. What information and reports do we need annually?	The strategic plan, with milestones The annual budget Management development and succession plans Health and safety review Risk assessment and control review The board effectiveness review
6. What do we need to ensure continued compliance with statutory obligations?	Annual review; annual checklist
7. When will we review remuneration?	Annually, with recommendations made to the board

Family companies

Family companies are worthy of special consideration. The challenges they face can be particularly tricky where more than one branch of the family have shareholdings and where several family members are involved in the management of the business.

Shareholders who have no part in the management of the company may well have the objective of crystallising the value of their shareholding and may, therefore, be focussed on an exit strategy. Management, on the other hand, may wish to preserve the heritage of the company and, indeed, their own executive roles. Good communication is essential in these circumstances. And a more formal and disciplined approach to meetings and governance may be necessary.

Crucially, family politicking should not be allowed to damage the business. A strong, independent non-executive will help keep the factions in check.

Set out in Figure 9.3 are some questions that will help clarify the position for family companies and make the relationships easier.

The story of a private, family business in Scotland, which, for the purposes of this book, I've called McTavish Ltd, further highlights the key issues. (See case study, pages 134 and 135.)

FIGURE 9.3
QUESTIONS FOR THE FAMILY BUSINESS

☐ Is everyone clear about the vision and mission of the company; have these been committed to writing and communicated to all shareholders and managers?

☐ Are there family members who wish over time to realise the value of their shareholdings? If yes, is there an agreed plan for achieving this?

☐ Is there a succession plan that shareholders as well as the board can commit to?

☐ Has the board appointed one or two independent directors who have the trust and respect of all shareholders?

☐ Where different branches of the family are involved in the management of the company, are job descriptions clear? Are there clear objectives and an appraisal process?

☐ Is there a clear policy for the resolution of family disputes?

☐ Is there a clear competency-based approach to employing new family members to defined roles that will add value to the company?

☐ Is there a distinction between business and family issues?

CASE STUDY: MCTAVISH LTD

The background

McTavish is a manufacturer of die castings for a variety of customers and industries. It was founded in 1975 by the then 30-year-old Hamish McTavish, who had worked in the metal bashing industry for 10 years.

McTavish saw the opportunity to make money in the die casting business, where the applications were relatively wide and labour costs relatively low. (Creation of the dies could be out-sourced.)

With initial capital of £5,000, half of which was borrowed, McTavish was able to set up a small operation consisting of an electric furnace and a four-slide small-product die casting machine. He already had a customer, who was prepared to give a long-term contract.

McTavish set up the plant in a small rented shed on an industrial site and outsourced the manufacture of the specialist dies to Germany. Once the dies were made, and the machines were set up, the production was automated. The ingots of zinc were conveyed to the furnace, melted and presented to the casting machine. Finished product was cooled and conveyed to packaging boxes.

The company supplied metal valves for bicycles and motorcycles, household goods and small components for motor industry contractors.

McTavish was a good employer who commanded the loyalty of his staff.

Soon, the large manufacturers in the motor industry, which had heard about his expertise and the quality of his products, offered him the chance to expand. They wanted bigger components, produced by bigger machines; and they wanted them to be supplied from key plants around the world.

Although McTavish was technically very able and read widely to keep up with new developments in the industry, he was an intuitive manager with no international experience.

If the expansion were to succeed the company would need not only new capital but also new skills.

The expansion programme

In 1987, McTavish made the decision to expand overseas and increase capacity in the UK. He drew up a seven-year expansion plan, which involved:

☐ a new, larger UK site;

☐ a plant in Germany;

☐ a plant in Mexico to feed the US motor vehicle market.

The funding gap was filled by a combination of private equity, debt and family money.

Filling the skills gap was arguably trickier. Hamish McTavish had a 17-year-old son Angus, who, he hoped, would one day take over the business. It was agreed, however, that Angus should first go to university to read business studies or economics.

It was clear that Hamish needed a right-hand person to manage the installation of the new operations and then to run the overseas interests. Further, it was felt that a wise non-executive director, who understood the industry and had experience of running international businesses, should be brought in. The private equity house also appointed a non-executive. The other directors were McTavish and his wife.

Hamish McTavish and his immediate family held 60 per cent of the shares; private equity 25 per cent; the wider family 15 per cent.

The stumbling blocks

During the seven-year plan, the business developed, but the learning curve was steep. Poor project-management skills meant delays and problems at each expansion. It was pretty much a case of "learning on the job" and dealing with the most pressing issues first. There were supply-chain and production problems.

McTavish's passion for quality, new technology and customer service remained, however, and probably saved the business.

McTavish drew satisfaction from the development of his business, but was growing increasingly more uncomfortable in the boardroom. Board meetings had changed beyond recognition. They were more formal, requiring papers to be prepared in advance and they were much more confrontational. The private equity investor interrogated Hamish, driven by the need for cash generation and the desire to exit the business in seven years, with a tax paid internal rate of return of between 25 per cent and 30 per cent.

The other non-executive director also proved incisive, keen to see proper standards of governance and to fulfil his role as business mentor.

Board meetings were not looked forward to by Mr and Mrs McTavish and, indeed, Mrs McTavish eventually stopped going to them.

Angus joined the company in 1992 after a business degree from Heriot-Watt University, but he did not seem to have the commitment and drive of his father. His role in the business was not clearly defined, and he was given a number of more short-term projects.

His strength lay in information technology; he disliked negotiation and confrontational meetings with the hard-nosed buyers in the motor industry.

Hamish continued to believe that Angus would take over the reins when he reached the age of 65 in 2005, putting his son's uncertainty in the business down to youth and inexperience.

CASE STUDY: MCTAVISH LTD (cont)

By 1994, however, the private equity holder was keen to realise its investment and it was clear that the McTavish family would not be able to make an attractive offer. The business had doubled in value over the past seven years and was, according to the accountant, now worth between £40m and £50m.

The private equity company had found a potential buyer in a major UK-based engineering conglomerate, which was expected to have significant synergies with McTavish Limited. On the basis of published information, the new company offered to buy out all shareholders at £60m. A two-year contract would be given to Hamish; but there was nothing on the table for Angus.

The outcome

Hamish was initially very resistant to the offer, keen to keep the business in the family.

After considerable discussion with the independent director, however, he understood that the offer was generous, and in the best interests of all shareholders, and that he had no right of veto as to who should run the company.

The offer was accepted, but Hamish stayed on less than six months. The manager he had appointed to run the overseas parts of the business was delighted that (with Angus out of the picture) he now had the opportunity for promotion, and stayed with the new owner.

Angus, who wanted to leave to join an IT firm, was equally happy.

The lessons

☐ Expansion plans create the need for a new capital structure.

☐ Moving from a small owner-manager model is a painful process; the skills required are seldom found in the company.

☐ Senior staff may be de-motivated by a succession plan of keeping the top job in the family.

☐ The children of founders do not necessarily have the skills for the future development of the business.

☐ More formality and process inevitably follow a widening of the shareholder base, and more time on governance and communication is necessary.

☐ A good independent director, who has the right skills and who is empathetic to the business, is valuable in the boardroom and as a mentor.

☐ Private equity holders will want an exit route and a high return in a defined period. This needs to be discussed up front, and the implications understood.

☐ Private equity houses may actively seek buyers for your business.

☐ A majority shareholding does not mean the right of veto.

Taking advice

Running a small business, of whatever type, is extremely demanding. The range of tasks is broad; the regulatory burden huge. Issues have to be faced that may have a fundamental impact on the business – and the owner-manager, founder or majority shareholder may often feel that they're facing them alone.

External advisers such as accountants, lawyers and banks are useful sources of specific information but they fall short of the more general "mentoring" or "coaching" role. They do not usually provide the kind of sounding boards SME directors need.

The gap can be filled in a number of ways.

- ☐ **Experienced non-executive directors** can be an invaluable addition to the board. As well as contributing to meetings, they will be available for off-the-record discussions and will provide the kind of input that makes executive decision-making more robust. As the Combined Code puts it, they will "constructively challenge" the board.

- ☐ The **accounting firm** can provide valuable insights. The partner concerned should have knowledge of the company, its competitors, the industry and the challenges that are faced. Relationships need to be built over time, if they are to provide the maximum value. (At the same time, of course, they must remain professional. Accountants and auditors who get too close to their clients or "go native" pose serious threats to internal control. This point is underlined in the Smith guidance in the Combined Code, which says that the provision of non-audit services by the auditor should not be allowed to impair their independence.)

- ☐ Directors can gain the benefit of wider experience by being involved in **industry groups or representative bodies** such as the IoD and the Federation of Small Businesses.

- ☐ Taking on a **non-executive role** in another, unrelated industry can help broaden the director's personal experience and increase their self-confidence.

Husband-and-wife teams

In some companies, the directors are husband and wife. Often, one runs the business as managing director; the other handles or assists with administration. This model may have tax benefits: if the less-involved party has no other income, they will be able to take tax-free cash up to the level of the personal allowance.

Sometimes, the husband will run the business and the wife will be a non-executive director. In these circumstances, it is important to remember that their duties and obligations will be the same under law.

The future of the business

For many small and family-run companies, change and growth can be painful. Those used to having and running their "own" businesses can find it difficult to adjust when a larger and different group of shareholders and stakeholders becomes involved. Nonetheless, the temptation to treat the company as their own personal fiefdom must be resisted. A fundamental principle of the law governing directors, remember, is that a company is a **separate legal entity**. There will need to be an understanding that there are important standards that apply with increasing weight as the business continues to grow.

Many owners of family businesses aim to develop the business over their working lives and then pass it on to their "heir". Indeed, children often grow up with the idea, carefully planted and repeated by the parent, that "one day all this will be theirs". The trouble is, the ideas and aspirations of parents and children often diverge. Inheritance does not, as the McTavish case study shows, constitute a good succession plan.

Where there is a happy congruence between the aspirations of parent and child, the child should still be encouraged to work outside the family business first. There is considerable merit in the ability to bring fresh ideas to the table, rather than simply copy the behaviours of the parent. In my view, the "heir" should be sent away for at least five years.

Some family owners recognise the frailty of the "inherited" management and look for professional outside managers to fill the top roles. This may well expand the company more readily and provide better balance and sub-division of responsibilities. Here, the owner manager needs to learn the art of delegation, an important component of effective leadership, discussed in detail in chapter 7.

Exit routes

During the strategic planning process, the owner needs to ask what their exit strategy is likely to be. If the answer is to continue trading for the next 20 years, then the question becomes, "How do we build value on the agreed basis set out in the strategic plan?"

If the business is capable of expanding at a faster rate, but lacks the management and/or cash resource to do so, further questions need to be asked:

☐ will the additional cash resource mean a dilution of family shareholdings, or, if debt is used, more restrictions by the lender?

☐ can new blood be brought into the business, motivated and retained to plug skills gaps?

☐ how will the owner adapt to working in a new way, with new people?

Some SME owners I've spoken to plan to exit the business in a much shorter timeframe, say between five and 10 years. Here the focus should still be:

☐ adding value in the time available;

☐ setting and following good standards of governance;

☐ having a management team that is capable of taking the business forward once the current owner has left.

Summary

The health of the economy is inextricably linked to the health of the SME sector. That's why SMEs have been given a separate chapter in this book.

There is real value to be harvested from good governance, irrespective of the size of your organisation. Effective directors of SMEs understand how the principles of best practice and good governance can be applied to add value to their companies.

Growth and expansion phases can expose management and structural weaknesses. Addressing these requires pragmatism and the ability to adapt.

Family businesses face particular challenges. Balancing the interests of family shareholders and those of the family members who run the company can be difficult. A clear strategy, clear communication and a disciplined approach to governance will help.

Succession plans must provide for the possibility that family members will be unwilling to take over the business or will lack the necessary skills. Pragmatism and adaptability are, again, key requirements.

charities and not-for-profit organisations

CHAPTER 10

Introduction

The idea that charities and other not-for-profit organisations (NPOs) are quaintly amateurish and run by volunteers of good intention but little ability is as false as it is patronising.

Charities are big business. The 200,000 in the UK have an annual income in excess of £25bn.

Over the past 10 or so years, the very large charities, perhaps the top five per cent, have adopted working practices similar to those of the commercial sector. There is a good reason for this: those who follow the principles of good corporate governance out-perform their peers.

A focus on good governance essentially means three things for charities and NPOs:

- [ ] the strategy, vision, mission and set of values to make decisions clearer and inspire employees, existing supporters and potential donors;

- [ ] the tools that provide objectivity for the board and help it fulfil its role and measure and monitor the organisation's progress;

- [ ] the transparency and integrity to win public and stakeholder trust and reassure donors that most of what they give goes directly to the cause they support.

Good governance, in other words, is as important for charities and NPOs as it is for commercial organisations.

This chapter aims to offer insights into the practices and processes that will add value and reduce risk. It will be a useful reference point for those who lead charities and NPOs or are thinking of joining them or setting them up.

It should not, however, be read in isolation. The principles of good governance are one of the main frames of reference for this book; there will be much of relevance elsewhere – particularly, perhaps, in chapters 1 to 5.

The legal framework

Before they look at the governance aspects of charities and NPOs, the trustees or directors must be clear about their legal duties and responsibilities.

A charity can take a number of legal forms, from a trust to an unincorporated organisation, or a company limited by guarantee. In addition, some are formed by Royal Charter or an Act of Parliament.

Each one will have a governing document, which may be a deed of trust or a memorandum and articles of association.

Further information on the legal position of trustees and directors of charities is given under the sections "the controlling body" and "incorporated charities" on pages 152 and 153. For a comprehensive guide to the legal and regulatory framework, however, the reader should consult *The ICSA Charity Trustee's Guide* by Jane Arnott, an excellent handbook for trustees.

The need for good governance

It is useful to examine the case for good governance in a more precise and detailed way.

Government and private-sector expectations

The worlds of the public sector and private enterprise often collide with the worlds of charities and NPOs.

Recent trends from around the world show, almost without exception, that governments are increasingly using NPOs to provide services in special areas such as healthcare and education. In the UK, for example, the government tackles inequalities in healthcare through Lottery-funded healthy living centres, which serve disadvantaged communities.

In the private sector, more and more businesses are using charities as their interface with the community. Their corporate social responsibility agenda increasingly includes joint projects with charities or support for specific initiatives within a charity's overall mission. Some companies release employees for community work – for example, helping children in local schools. Some will nominate a "charity of the year" and organise fund-raising events. Others will liaise through high-profile sponsorship deals.

Funds provided by the government or by the commercial sector are increasingly dependent upon high levels of governance and total transparency. They are unlikely to given where there are serious concerns about the way a charity or NPO is being run.

Charities will need to reassure large-scale benefactors and the government, through transparent audit trails, that funds have been efficiently used for the designated cause. They will also need to reassure them that the quality of the board is high and that the key governance processes are in place.

Public expectations

The demand for good governance is also "consumer" or community-led.

Public concerns about organisations and their leaders have serious implications for a sector that depends on goodwill. Potential donors and volunteers (the public at large) will have asked themselves a number of questions.

- ☐ Why do we see examples of failures when there is no apparent warning?
- ☐ How can audited accounts be so far from the reality? How can frauds and misreporting be possible?
- ☐ Why do charities sometimes lose value through investment policies?
- ☐ Why do charities seem to spend our donations on a very narrow aspect of the work they're committed to?
- ☐ Why do payments to directors sometimes seem excessive and unrelated to the value they create?
- ☐ How do we know that most of what we give to a charity will go to the charitable cause?

Some of these concerns can be addressed by better communication; others require appropriate standards to be set and supported within the organisation.

It is clear, though, that failure to address them is not an option. Without public support, funds dwindle, volunteer numbers shrink and charities fail.

Senior-employee expectations

The not-for-profit sector is increasingly hiring its senior people from the private sector.

Directors from commercial backgrounds increasingly serve both in an executive or non-executive capacity in government-sponsored quangos or agencies. These people expect, and will be used to, good standards of governance.

Charities and NPOs will find it more difficult to compete in the labour market if they don't have the correct systems and structures in place.

Macro-economic trends

Charities and NPOs are not immune to economic fluctuations. An effective monitoring system, one of the cornerstones of good governance, will pick up negative trends early and allow remedial action to be taken.

The case for good governance is, therefore, compelling. It will lead to better practice, more effective control, better people performance, and it will give reassurance to donors and supporters.

The precise degree of application and the formality of the processes will depend on the size and complexity of the charity.

What makes for good governance?

Good governance is clearly the lifeblood of charities and NPOs. But what exactly *is* it? The key principles have been stated many times in this book. But they bear repeating.

Governance is about understanding and managing the risks, ensuring that there are the right checks and balances for boardroom and executive power, and that the values of the organisation are fully supported and practised.

There are still many in the commercial sector and the government and not-for-profit sector who see governance as something that they need to conform to, as a "box-ticking" exercise. This is negative and limited thinking. Good governance adds real value. This applies in all sectors.

Good governance is not just about setting down a framework of rules and regulations. It is about the **essence and the culture of the organisation**. It is only effective when it is second nature, when it is an attitude of mind.

The essentials for this sector are:

☐ a clear sense of purpose and focus on the space the NPO occupies;

☐ clarity of strategy and certainty of values;

☐ a clear constitution, highlighting the purpose, powers, and obligations of the organisation;

☐ a clear understanding of the role of the board of trustees and those items reserved for its decision-making, and of the division of responsibilities between chairman and CEO;

☐ a control environment that gives assurance to the trustees that the accounts are correctly drawn up, and that the opportunity for fraud or other loss is kept to acceptable levels;

☐   agreement as to the information the board needs to monitor the health of the NPO and the frequency with which it should be provided;

☐   the appointment of a suitably qualified and independent auditor;

☐   an annual process for assessing risks and ensuring that they are being managed in an appropriate way;

☐   where investments are held, an investment policy agreed by the trustees that recognises the financial needs of the NPO and the risks attached to different classes of assets (see "investments", page 149).

FIGURE 10.1
HIGH-LEVEL AREAS OF FOCUS

☐ Does the constitution clearly state the areas for charitable support?

☐ Is the distinction between the roles of chief executive and chairman of the board clear and understood?

☐ Has the board debated and agreed the values for the organisation?

☐ Does the board have a clear schedule of items reserved for its decision-making?

☐ Does the board regularly review its membership, its effectiveness and the contribution it makes?

☐ Is there a satisfactory segregation of duties, especially in relation to financial matters?

☐ Have management and the board undertaken a risk assessment and control exercise? Is the board satisfied that the high-level risks have been identified and managed?

☐ Is there a clear policy on investments and the monitoring of their performance? Has relative risk been factored into this? Does the board regularly review this?

☐ Does the board have sufficient information to enable it to monitor progress against a pre-determined plan? And is this information received promptly?

☐ Has an independent auditor been appointed, and is there a direct interface between the board (or its audit committee) and the auditor?

☐ Are there clear procedures for ensuring that all income is banked and payments correctly paid?

☐ Is there a transparent arms-length process to review the remuneration of the staff?

☐ Is there a "whistle-blowing" procedure?

☐ Have all the statutory requirements been met?

Putting the building blocks in place: start at the top

As with most things, good standards of governance start at the top. They must be an agenda item for the board of trustees; they must be enthusiastically embraced by the chief executive; and they must be reflected in the values of the organisation.

The actions of members of the board must be consistent with the values and the standards of governance of the organisation.

Figure 10.1 lists the areas that the board and chief executive should address.

Values

In many organisations, the level of commitment to values is low. Yet values, if set down, communicated and practised, are the soul of the organisation and provide guidance to employees and volunteers about how they are expected to act. The most helpful sets of values are clear and concise. Figure 10.2 sets out a statement of values for a hypothetical charity in the field of cancer research.

FIGURE 10.2
VALUES FOR A CHARITY

1. Our primary focus is cancer research. We will be well informed about the trends and the opportunities in this field and understand the extent of (and limitations to) the contribution we can make.

2. In all that we do, we will hold ourselves accountable to the highest standards, so that we can be sure we are maximising our effectiveness and reassure the community. We will be professional in all that we do.

3. Our lifeblood is the contributions we receive from the community. We will communicate freely, and treat every donor as special.

4. The impact we make depends upon the people in our organisation. All our people must feel valued and enabled to contribute to the highest level possible. We will provide training and development for them, ensuring that no-one is disadvantaged on the grounds of sex, race, or disability.

5. Our organisation must be open and honest, sharing information that will help us be more effective. High integrity is an essential for all our people; and must be demonstrated in our actions.

6. We must be cost-effective in our operations, delivering the maximum proportion possible of funds raised to our chosen cause.

7. Our reputation in the community is critical, and we will do all that we can to enhance it.

Clarity

Clarity is needed to avoid a muddled organisation and weakened governance. The board needs to be clear about those items reserved for its approval or consideration, and there should be clear definition of the roles of chairman and chief executive.

The first step is for the board to set down a list of "reserved matters". These will vary according to the exact requirements of the organisation, but Figure 10.3 below can be used as a starting point.

The second step is to set out the roles of chairman and chief executive in job descriptions that are approved by the board. It is inefficient to have overlap, and potentially harmful to have underlap of duties and responsibilities.

The job description should, for the sake of clarity, avoid unnecessary detail. Figure 10.4 sets out a sample job description for the chairman of a charity, based on the essential requirements of the role.

FIGURE 10.3
MATTERS RESERVED FOR THE BOARD OF TRUSTEES

The board shall consider and agree the strategy and the resources needed to deliver it.

The board shall agree the operating plan and the budget for each year.

Any material changes to the scope of the charity or the direction of its support will be agreed by the board.

The board will agree changes to board membership and the top executive team in advance.

The board will monitor and evaluate the performance of the chief executive, and ensure that the top team has an appropriate process for setting and monitoring objectives.

The board will monitor the progress of the charity against the pre-determined plan. It will satisfy itself as to the adequacy and timeliness of the information it receives to do this.

The board will approve major investments and capital items, and will review the delivery of them against the original plans.

The board will consider the high-level risks in the business and the plans to control them.

The board will approve the published accounts.

The board will consider any major communication programme with the public to ensure that the tone is consistent with the ideals and values of the charity.

The board shall be satisfied that the control environment is appropriate and robust.

FIGURE 10.4
JOB DESCRIPTION FOR THE CHAIR OF A CHARITY

Primary objective

☐ To provide the overall leadership, in close co-operation with the chief executive, in a way that maximises the contribution of the trustees and the staff, and donations from the target community. To ensure that all concerned are focused on achieving the charity's goals.

Specific duties

☐ Ensuring that there is balance on the board, with the right mix of skills and experience

☐ Establishing clear procedures for rotation on the board, for the identification of new trustees and for their appointment

☐ Ensuring that there is a succession plan both for the board and for the senior executive team

☐ Participating actively in strategy formation prior to it being presented to the board

☐ Monitoring and acting as a mentor to the chief executive

☐ Establishing appropriate sub-committees

☐ Assisting, where appropriate, with contact with key donors or potential donors, and with any other PR activities

☐ Chairing the board

☐ Ensuring that there is an annual board appraisal process

Other duties

☐ Appraising the chief executive annually, and ensuring that there is a process to set objectives for and appraise all staff

☐ Ensuring that there is an induction and a training programme for new trustees and that they are fully aware of any areas where improvement is needed

☐ Ensuring that the control environment is satisfactory

Investments

Many charities and NPOs choose to invest substantial donations – e.g. bequests from wealthy benefactors. This is not the place to offer a detailed treatise on the management of investments and the various options available. However, there are some key principles that need to be borne in mind.

☐   First is the need to spread risk. Having a block of shares in one company designed to provide both a stream of dividends and capital appreciation is fine if the company outperforms the index, less so if the reverse occurs. Selling the shares at a good time in the market can allow for a more balanced portfolio: the proceeds can be re-invested in a group of companies.

☐   Second is the need to hold an appropriate balance of types of investment. Although equities have outperformed fixed-interest investments (e.g. gilts) over time, they present a higher risk to both income and capital. There is always a risk-reward trade-off; the trustees will have to decide just how safe they want to play. **The cash needs of the organisation will be a primary consideration.** If a life insurance company were providing an annuity or a pension, for example, it would buy fixed-interest assets to ensure the annual liability was matched by the income receivable.

In the past few years, we've seen charities' spending plans slashed due to a decline in income or asset values. Balancing investments to match the charity's needs, and paying careful consideration to the risk profiles of investment vehicles, is essential.

Starting up

Requirements

The developed world is well served by charities and it's hard to think of a cause that isn't represented. Therefore, the first question that any would-be charity promoter should ask is, "What space will this charity occupy?" The promoter needs to understand the competitive environment and how the proposed new charity will differentiate itself.

The early analysis will reflect the appeal of the key aims and objectives, as this will directly influence the ability to raise money.

The size of the fund needed to carry out the work and the "back-office" support to run the organisation will influence the key cost-to-serve (expenses-to-revenue) ratio, and this, too, will influence a potential donor. No-one wants to make gifts to charities that spend a high proportion of their income on support costs.

Once the operating space has been identified and agreed, it is helpful to set down an operating charter covering the **vision, mission and values** of the charity.

Vision, mission and values have been discussed in detail elsewhere in this book (e.g. chapters 1 and 3). They arguably, though, have additional force and meaning when applied to an organisation that exists to do good.

The vision is the inspiring view of what the charity can become. It is the visualisation of its future shape and success.

It describes the reason for the organisation's existence. It should be an inspirational statement that explains the purpose of the charity and how it expects to achieve excellence and competitive differentiation. The very best statements start with a clear idea of where the organisation is today and where it wants to be tomorrow. People and potential donors have a greater chance of being inspired if the statement is short, clear and represents a rallying cry.

The mission describes what needs to be done to achieve the envisioned state. It is a directional road map and sets milestones for the "strategic journey".

The values are the glue that holds the organisation together. It is a short list of things that are really important in decision-making for the charity. In other words, it is a set of principles and standards of conduct that need to be embedded in the organisation.

Formalities

Setting up a charity, like setting up a business, requires groundwork and preparation.

One of the first tasks is to draw up a constitution. Typically, this will describe the scope of the charity and the rules by which it will be run. It should make clear where the charity's main interests lie without imposing rigid constraints.

The constitution is a key document in obtaining charitable status; a key point of reference for the charity commissioners.

Once charitable status has been granted, the organisation will need to be registered with the tax authorities so that tax breaks can be claimed. It will also need to choose a bank – on criteria such as cost, service and interest paid on cash balances.

The appointment of an auditor should be given serious consideration. A good auditor will give assurance to stakeholders and add value by making recommendations for improving the control environment.

Premises should be selected on the basis of organisational need as well as cost. While it is important not to spend more than is necessary and to keep fixed costs and overheads down, choosing the cheapest option may be false economy. We all need a reasonable and effective environment for our staff. While I do not support unwarranted cost, I do believe that charities sometimes err on the side of what's frugal rather than what's pragmatic.

Choosing the organisation

Aims and aspirations can only be delivered through having the right people in the right place – in an organisation that is *shaped to deliver*.

The right organisational structure is one that:

☐   is simple, clear and commensurate with the size of the charity;

☐   meets strategic and operating needs effectively;

☐   has short lines of decision-making, workable spans of control for the key job holders;

☐   is cost-effective;

☐   has a clear division of power at the top, with checks and balances that provide an effective framework for governance.

The controlling body

All charities will need a governing body, and this is often called the board of trustees.

Trustees of charities differ in kind from directors of commercial enterprises – the great majority will be volunteers and receive no payment for their work – but their basic duties and responsibilities are strikingly similar.

The Charity Commission describes their role like this: "Trustees must accept ultimate responsibility for directing the affairs of a charity and ensuring that it is solvent, well-run and delivering the charitable outcomes for the benefit of the public for which it has been set up".

Substitute "charity" with "company", "charitable outcomes" with "strategy" and "public" with "shareholders and stakeholders" and you could be talking about the role of company directors.

Just like company directors, the trustees are **fiduciaries**. They must only use the funds and assets of the organisation in furtherance of the objectives laid down in its constitution. And just like company directors, they must ensure compliance with relevant law and regulation, and prepare reports and annual returns and accounts. **(The principal statutory instrument is the Charities Act 1993; the regulator is the Charity Commission.)**

The board of trustees will:

- [ ] set the long-term strategy for the organisation and monitor the performance of the chief executive and the executive team in the attainment of the agreed milestones;

- [ ] agree senior appointments and remuneration of the key employees;

- [ ] ensure that the key people enhance the reputation of the charity and live by and live up to its values.

A chairman will need to be appointed to lead the trustees. (See "choosing trustees" on the next page for more details on board composition etc.)

Incorporated charities

Some charities are registered with Companies House as well as the Charity Commission. Where this is the case, the charity is a **separate legal entity**, and its trustees are treated in law as company directors.

Registration with Companies House has the advantage of limited liability; it means the trustees will not be asked to make up the shortfall if the charity's liabilities exceed its assets. It is often the preferred model for larger charities with more complex asset bases.

(Charities incorporated by Royal Charter or statute are *not* registered with Companies House.)

Information for the board

The reporting system must be capable of providing information that enables both the executive team and the board of trustees to monitor progress.

The information must be supplied in good time, allowing warning signs to be given and corrective action to be taken when plans go awry.

And it must cover more than the straight financials. The board, for example, will want to measure:

- [ ] donor attitudes (e.g. through surveys);
- [ ] market share;
- [ ] conversion rates for donors;
- [ ] the effectiveness of charitable spending.

In larger organisations, there should also be measures for employee satisfaction – e.g. staff turnover and absenteeism rates – and reports on training and development.

Choosing trustees

Composition of the board

Choosing the individuals who will act as trustees and be members of the board is a serious and important business. The trustees must be sympathetic to the aims of the charity, and between them have the various skills sets that make an effective team. The best teams avoid "group think" and invite challenges but are mutually supportive, with a good balance of skills and experience. The members should be well-informed and work effectively together. The performance of the team as a whole should be greater than the sum of its parts. The points on boardroom effectiveness made in chapter 1 and elsewhere in this book apply equally well here.

The size of the board will obviously depend on the size of the organisation. The rule of thumb, though, is for there to be minimum of three members, two of whom should be **independent**.

Ideally, the composition of the board should be balanced not only in terms of the members' skills and experience but also their **independence and non-independence**. There are some foundations where the benefactor wishes to have a significant say in the running of the charity and where they wish to be on the board. Other trustees are often appointed because they know the benefactor well and are likely to be supportive of his or her wishes. While there is nothing inherently wrong with this approach, it does carry risks; support and sycophancy sometimes get confused.

In my experience, there is great value in having trustees who are truly independent, who can exercise sound judgment, who collectively have wider experience than the benefactor and their "circle", and who can provide constructive criticism.

A chairman will be appointed to lead this well-balanced board of trustees. Best practice suggests that the appointments of the chairman and all trustees should be for a **finite period**. The norm for commercial independent directors in a company is for a term of three years, with the prospect of renewal for a further three-year period. This is a reasonable model for the not-for-profit sector, too, but the chair should ensure that there is a reasonable rotation of trustees. There is great inefficiency if all trustees have common terms and all need to be rotated at the same time.

Skills sets on the board

A fundamental requirement will be understanding of the **stewardship role of trustees**. The members of the board need to:

- [ ] ensure that that the charity stays **true to the principal cause** for which it has been formed;

- [ ] protect the longevity of the charity and its aims, objectives and principles; ensure that the charity and its ethos outlast its founders/key people.

At the same time, however, there is a requirement on the board for **financial literacy**. The trustees must (collectively if not individually) also be able to protect the efficiency of the organisation so that it is run in a cost-effective way and, crucially, so that the maximum amount of money raised is spent on the good cause.

More and more donors, especially the larger benefactors, are demanding transparency, value for money and clear risk control. They want the board to achieve maximum value from hard-won funds.

A parallel trend is for a greater proportion of trustees to come from the commercial sector.

The march of business has caused disquiet in some quarters, with chairmen of charities claiming that it risks alienating existing and potential donors. The observation I would make is that the remit of business people is not to *commercialise* charities but to help them to operate to the highest possible standards.

Charities are different from profit-making businesses but they have many of the same needs: clear direction and leadership, effective oversight and efficiency.

A diversity of backgrounds among trustees is a strength, leading to better and more informed decisions.

A trustee's perspective

Selection should, of course, be two-way. The role of trustee is demanding, onerous and, as we've seen, usually unpaid. The candidate will want to feel that this is an organisation that they believe in and will feel proud to work for.

Before taking on the job of trustee, I ask myself a number of questions.

- [ ] Do I fully understand the scope of the charity and am I enthused by its work?

- [ ] Do I really think that I can make a difference? Or is the organisation just looking for someone to make up the numbers?

- [ ] Can I give the required time?

- [ ] Does the board provide the leadership required and have an agenda that is relevant?

- [ ] Will I look forward to the meetings and to the information flow from them?

FIGURE 10.5
HEALTH CHECK FOR CHARITIES AND NPOs

Scoring: + 3 for definite yes; +1 for qualified yes; -2 for definite no

Purpose
1. Is there a clear understanding of the purpose, direction and values?
2. Can the trustees identify with the charity's aims?
3. Is the charity sufficiently differentiated from others in its field?

The board of trustees
4. Is the balance on the board right? (Skills and experience)
5. Does the board provide the required leadership?
6. Is the agenda comprehensive and appropriate?
7. Is sufficient information available?
8. Does the board pay sufficient attention to its own governance? (Authority levels and self-appraisal)

The management
9. Are there clear objectives, and is progress against them monitored?
10. Are appraisals open, effective and two-way?
11. Are managers selected objectively against the job requirements?
12. Is training available to meet needs identified?

The workforce and voluntary workers
13. Do they feel valued and fully involved?
14. Is there good communication with all sectors, and are key messages fully understood?
15. Does this charity select the most suitable people rather than those who happen to be available?
16. Is there an open culture, where challenge and improvement are sought out?

General
17. Does the organisation allow people to contribute to the full level of their ability?
18. Is there a clear understanding of the purpose, direction and values?
19. Is management alert to new trends and external factors that will influence future direction?
20. Is the organisation seen as a great place to work?

Evaluation: 40 and above Exceptional; 33-39 Excellent; 26-32 Good, but there are areas that need attention; 19-25 Significant improvements are needed; less than 19 Unsatisfactory

☐   Are the professional standards high, is good governance in place, is reputation good?

☐   Do I like the team of people, and respect their views? Do they find time for fun?

Candidates will also want to establish what their liabilities will be – i.e. whether or not the charity is incorporated/a limited liability company.

In deciding whether or not to continue with their role, trustees will need to think about the effectiveness of the organisation. Figure 10.5 provides a health check for not-for-profit organisations. It is meant as a general template and may have to be adapted to reflect the specific needs of the organisation.

It has a scoring mechanism based on established norms.

Smaller charities

Definition

Small charities are those with income or expenditure of less than £20,000 a year. They are subjected to a relatively light regulatory regime by the Charity Commission and may file abbreviated reports and accounts, and simplified annual returns.

"Smaller" charities can be defined as those with income up to £250,000.

Is there a difference?

In the course of preparation for this book, a wide range of not-for-profit organisations have been approached for their views. The smaller charities had concerns about the cost implications of following what is perceived as best practice.

The key to effectiveness is to ensure that the essential building blocks are in place but that red tape and processes are kept to a minimum. Governance need not be a cost or administrative burden.

The founder or current head should decide which things are vital for the efficient and effective running of the charity.

Figure 10.6 lists the processes that are regarded as the minimum for smaller charities.

Some of the entries in Figure 10.6 need further comment.

The governing document, **the constitution**, will have been drawn up at the time of the charity's formation. There will, however, be a periodic need to review it for continued relevance.

Charities with only a few staff often question the need for a formal laying down of their purpose, direction and values. Stating the **vision and mission** of the organisation not only adds to clarity and focus but is also a valuable communications tool for potential donors. Stating the **values** can be put off when the charity is in its infancy, but will be essential once more staff and volunteers start to be recruited.

The accounting system need not be complex but it must be robust and allow progress to be monitored accurately.

Although smaller charities are not legally required to appoint an independent auditor, best practice suggests they should. As we've seen, an auditor can add value and provide the assurance so crucial for stakeholders and donors.

The auditor will need to be satisfied that all income received is properly accounted for, that expenditure is within the terms of the constitution and that all charitable disbursements are for causes specified. The assets and liabilities will be scrutinised so that the balance sheet can be certified as presenting a true and fair view at the specified date. The controls will be reviewed to ensure that they are satisfactory.

FIGURE 10.6
ESSENTIALS FOR SMALLER CHARITIES

- [ ] An up-to date constitution
- [ ] Registration with the Charity Commission and the Inland Revenue
- [ ] Clarity of purpose and direction, set down formally and reviewed annually *(A values statement is only optional where there are only a few employees or volunteers)*
- [ ] A board of no fewer than three trustees, two of whom should be independent
- [ ] An independent auditor *(obligatory for charities with income in excess of £250,000)*
- [ ] Accounting and legal controls commensurate with the organisation's size
- [ ] A strategy for fund raising
- [ ] An annual budget and operating plan
- [ ] Financial reporting that, at least every six months, compares actual results against the plan
- [ ] Compliance with legal and regulatory obligations, including Charity Commission filing requirements
- [ ] Where income from investments help fund the charity, a formal investment policy

The public sector

Governments have been keen to introduce private-sector discipline to public-sector organisations. Nonetheless, the challenges for directors working in these organisations remain great.

Interference from officials and politicians means decision-making can be painfully slow. Targets set by government may be contradictory or seem to fly in the face of commercial common sense. And, when things go wrong, the law of "spin" means the board, rather than the minister and their aides, is the first to be blamed.

This may sound like a daunting (even alien) environment for company directors, but there is a real need for their expertise, patience and determination to be used for the benefit of the community. The principles for success are really quite straightforward and differ only in a small way from the principles required by a commercial organisation.

There is a need for:

- ☐ a clear vision, mission and values;
- ☐ clear objectives for those delivering them, ensuring, through the cascading down of these objectives, that there is a common goal and clear co-operation between the different parts of the organisation;
- ☐ good communications across the organisation and to all stakeholders, including the community being served;
- ☐ regular board meetings and regular meetings with the relevant politicians to share progress and build trust;
- ☐ a high-calibre board with the right balance of skills and strong leadership from the chairman;
- ☐ an appropriate and timely flow of information to the board to enable progress to be monitored and risks to be identified and managed;
- ☐ an annual board effectiveness review.

Despite the difficulties, this can be a rewarding sector for the conscientious and committed director.

Sir Hugh Sykes, a board member of the Institute of Directors, has helped transform the Mid Yorkshire Hospitals Trust, bringing to the role of chairman not only diligence and hard work but also the principles outlined above.

A case study on the trust makes a fitting end to this chapter.

CASE STUDY: MID YORKSHIRE HOSPITALS TRUST

The background

By 2004, both the finances and clinical performance of the Mid Yorkshire Hospitals Trust (MYHT) were giving cause for serious concerns.

The trust, which covers hospitals in Dewsbury, Wakefield and Pontefract, had an income/expenditure deficit of £30m a year and total debts of £60m. Its services were deemed unsatisfactory in two areas of medicine. Its relationship with the local authority was weak, and proposals to build two new hospitals had been rejected. The board had little control over operations. The trust was reputed to be one of the worst, if not the worst, in the country.

In late 2004, MYHT became the first NHS trust to be put into "special measures" by the Healthcare Commission in order to monitor and improve its performance.

The underlying problems

A recent Audit Commission report suggested that there are usually three things that lead hospital trusts into difficulties. These are:

☐ mergers with other hospitals;

☐ Private Finance Initiative (PFI) projects;

☐ re-configuration of hospital services, requiring discussions with local stakeholders as well as with the regional health authority, MPs, local authorities, unions etc.

All three of the above applied to MYHT. Hospital mergers had met integration problems. Proposals to build two new hospitals to replace antiquated buildings in Wakefield and Pontefract under the PFI had, for more than 10 years, met "complications". The most recent had failed on the grounds that they were too expensive. Revised proposals (which would cost just as much and provide fewer beds) had been accepted by the strategic health authority (SHA) but had yet to be finalised with the Department of Health. Contract signature looked a long way off.

Re-configuration plans, necessary for the effective and efficient running of the trust's services, had led to ill-feeling among local stakeholders.

The solutions

A new chairman, new chief executive and a new board were brought in to work out what had to be done.

Their priorities were clear:

☐ financial turnaround;

☐ re-organisation of medical departments;

☐ conclusion of the PFI negotiations;

☐ resolving the configuration issues.

Financial turnaround – A director was appointed to lead the financial turnaround, with help from a Department of Health central team. A plan was agreed and implemented.

The 5,000-strong workforce was re-organised, and 450 posts were lost. The process was difficult, but conducted with complete openness. It resulted in but 10 compulsory redundancies; the rest of the staff were redeployed and found new posts.

The use of outside and agency staff was severely curtailed.

Detailed plans were discussed with the medical directorates, and the level of co-operation was on the whole excellent.

As the financial turnaround was taking place, additional costs were loaded on to the organisation, making the maintenance of morale difficult. Nonetheless, the agreed plan was carried through.

Reorganisation of some medical practices – A new medical director was appointed, and assistance given by a central Department of Health resource.

Medical services and outcomes are now a major part of board agendas.

PFI – The key to securing the PFI deals was clear identification of priorities and timescales, and additional resources.

The chairman became personally involved; and new people were recruited.

Negotiations were not easy, but were eventually brought to a satisfactory close.

Re-configuration – Paying for the new hospitals would mean re-configuration of services. Rather than discuss every possible eventuality in detail, however, the board decided the priority should be to avoid further (expensive) delays and get the new hospitals up and running. The important thing was to have new, up-to-date facilities that could be adapted easily to changing circumstances and needs.

Board operation

It was clear that the above objectives could not be achieved without better discipline on the board. The frequency of meetings was increased from bi-monthly to monthly, with good papers submitted in advance.

The lessons

The turnaround of an NHS trust has much in common with the turnaround of a private enterprise. It depends on:

- an understanding of costs;
- a focus on the key issues;
- understanding the areas for improvement;
- the right skills and resources – in the right quantity;
- clear identification of priorities.

The caveats

Anyone entering the health service from a private-sector background has to be prepared for a number of frustrations.

- The interests of politicians can impede decision-making and lead to delays. Risk-taking is very difficult. (If one strives for 90 per cent efficiency in the private sector, a realistic aim in the public sector would be 70 per cent.)
- The financial penalties for sub-standard performance are not as draconian as they are in the private sector. (Unlike an entrepreneur or a business, the government can't go bust.)
- Attempts to direct operations from the centre can make "internal" responsibilities and accountabilities unclear and can de-motivate staff.
- The need to consult a high number of different stakeholders/interest groups can distract management from the primary task of providing the best possible affordable care for patients.

The outcome

Despite the above, working in and helping lead a NHS Trust can be immensely satisfying. There is a high number of highly dedicated, highly skilled and able people in the service. And they can produce outstanding results.

MYHT came out of special measures in 2006. It is (at the time of writing) working to a detailed plan to break even in 2007/8.

The Healthcare Commission and the secretary of state have congratulated the trust on the speed and completeness of the turnaround.

Reproduced with kind permission of Sir Hugh Sykes

Summary

Charities and NPOs make an increasingly important contribution to both society and the economy. Successive governments have placed more responsibilities on their shoulders.

The growth in size and importance of the sector has led to new standards of "professionalism", the core of which are the principles of good governance.

Following these principles will give assurance to stakeholders, benefactors and supporters that the appropriate controls and checks and balances are in place.

Governance demands certain formalities and procedures – for example, effective supply of information for the board – but these should reflect the needs and size of the organisation. Unnecessary process and complexity are the enemies of good governance. Governance should add value to the organisation, not impede its progress.

The critical areas that will add value to charities and NPOs include:

- risk assessment and control;

- clear strategic planning and performance monitoring;

- a clear and clearly communicated vision and mission and (for larger charities, at least) set of values;

- careful selection of the board of trustees and a clear understanding of duties, responsibilities and division of power on the board.

The story of the turnaround of the Mid Yorkshire Hospitals Trusts, included at the end of this chapter, shows how the principles of good corporate governance, practised by commercial organisations, can be used to add value in the public sector.

For directors from commercial backgrounds, moving into the not-for-profit sector can be something of a "culture shock". This, however, should not be allowed to overshadow the fact that they can make a real difference.

ethics

CHAPTER 11

Introduction

Effective directors are, as we've seen, guided by strong and clear values. In all but the smallest organisations, these will be committed to writing and promulgated. Clearly communicated to and fully understood by all employees, they become *embedded* in the organisation.

This chapter explores the complementary dimension of ethics – the moral principles that must govern business behaviour.

The case for ethics

The idea that principles hold a business back, that success is always linked to "sharp practice", that business people must push moral boundaries if they are to make money for themselves and their shareholders is wrong.

Increasing numbers of businesses are making values and ethics part of their USP. Cafédirect is the "UK's largest Fairtrade hot drinks company"; Freeplay Energy is the "leading global brand of clean, dependable energy products"; Innocent Drinks wants to "leave things a little better" than it finds them, making products that are "100 per cent good for people" from ingredients that are "procured ethically", minimising its carbon footprint and giving 10 per cent of its profits to charities in its suppliers' communities.

These relatively young companies are in tune with the *zeitgeist* but they shouldn't be seen purely as products of their own time. They're part of a tradition of principled business. Think Rowntree, think Cadbury, think John Spedan Lewis in the UK. All were philanthropists; all built profitable businesses.

The most precious asset any leader has is their good name. The same is true of their "host" organisation – be it a business, a not-for-profit organisation or a charitable foundation. When reputations are lost, so too is value. Sales and share prices fall. Nike, engulfed by a sweatshop scandal in the 1990s, is just one company to have discovered this.

Good names are rarely built on bad behaviour.

What are ethics?

Some writers spend a great deal of time explaining the difference between values and ethics. But most would probably agree that in one important respect at least they're the same: they're both essential elements of effective leadership.

FIGURE 11.1
WORD PICTURE FOR BUSINESS VALUES AND ETHICS

Words to describe business values	Words to describe ethics
Customer service	Highest ethical standards
Efficiency	Integrity
Good governance	Honesty
Reliability	Responsibility
Profitability	Respect
Teamwork	Trust
Quality	Fairness
Value for money	Openness
Initiative	Transparency
Shareholder value	*(With kind permission of IBE)*

If you qualify the word values by the word "moral", you can see how closely related the two concepts are: **moral values = ethics**.

If you qualify it by the word "business", things get more complicated – but not *that* much.

The Institute of Business Ethics (IBE) sets out common words that describe business values and ethical values. These are listed in Figure 11.1 above.

On the left, we have a list of those things that will be important to a business – *what it values*. They are the cultural norms of the organisation. On the right, are the qualities or behavioural standards important in observing/maintaining them. You can't, for example, have effective teamwork or customer service without integrity, respect, fairness and trust.

Ethical business: the starting point

Most FTSE 350 companies have a statement of ethical behaviour. This reinforces the values of the organisation and sets out the moral code for employees. In many businesses, it supports and supplements the CSR agenda.

A code is essential for any organisation with 50 or more employees, but it will be meaningless unless:

☐   directors (or their equivalents) lead by example;

☐   the standards are practised and enforced.

The "nice words" of the statement must have a life beyond paper. An organisation must practise what it preaches. If it doesn't, the main effect of the statement will be to expose its leaders as hypocrites.

This was amply demonstrated by the case of Enron and Kenneth Lay.

Enron had a detailed and theoretically excellent code of ethics, which set out how the corporation was to be run. Lay, then chairman and chief executive officer, introduced it in 2000 with these words:

"We want to be proud of Enron and know that it enjoys a reputation for fairness and honesty and that it is respected. Gaining such respect is one aim of our advertising and public relations activities, but no matter how effective they may be, Enron's reputation finally depends on its people, on you and me. Let's keep that reputation high."

The very next year, Enron collapsed under a mountain of "hidden" debts, and Lay and fellow director Jeff Skilling faced allegations of fraud.

Exhortation is not enough. It must be fully supported by action.

What should a code include?

Bearing in mind the caveats above, it will be useful to examine the contents of an ethical code. This is best done by way of an example, and I include, at Figure 11.2, the Code of Ethics for Biocon.

This states that the code applies universally, sets out the ethical standards, emphasises that they should be followed in the *spirit* as well as in the letter of the law, and provides a mechanism for reporting any failures.

Biocon is an Indian company, employing around 1,000 people. But I believe its code is a template for any organisation that takes ethics seriously.

Key principles

Some of the main elements of and principles behind the Biocon code are looked at more closely on pages 169 and 170. They are the key components of business ethics.

FIGURE 11.2
CODE OF ETHICS AND BUSINESS CONDUCT, BIOCON INDIA

This code is applicable to all directors, officers and employees of Biocon Ltd and its subsidiaries

Biocon Group is committed to conducting its business in accordance with the applicable laws, rules and regulations and with the highest standards of business ethics. This code is intended to provide guidance and help in recognising and dealing with ethical issues, provide mechanisms to report unethical conduct and help foster a culture of honesty and accountability. Each director, officer and employee is expected to comply with the letter and spirit of the code.

All employed in the company must not only comply with applicable laws, rules and regulations but should also promote honest and ethical conduct of the business. They must abide by the policies and procedures that govern the conduct of the company's business. Their responsibilities include helping to create and maintain a culture of high ethical standards and commitment to compliance, and to maintain a work environment that encourages stakeholders to raise concerns for the attention of management.

This code does not attempt to describe all potential problem areas that could develop, but some of the more common are described below.

Conflicts of interest

These can arise from:

- action or interests that may make it difficult for employees, officers and directors to perform their work pragmatically and effectively;
- the receipt of improper personal benefits as a result of one's position in the company (including benefits for family members);
- an outside business activity that detracts from an individual's ability to devote appropriate time and attention to their responsibilities in the company;
- the receipt of non-nominal gifts or excessive entertainment from any person or company with which Biocon has current or prospective business;
- any significant ownership interest in a supplier, customer, development partner or competitor of the company;
- any consulting or employment relationship with any supplier, customer, development partner or competitor.

All employed by the company should be scrupulous in avoiding conflicts of interest. Where there is likely to be a conflict of interest, the person concerned should make full disclosure of all facts and circumstances to the board of directors or to the committee or officer nominated for this purpose, and prior written approval should be obtained.

Honest and ethical conduct

The directors, officers and employees shall act in accordance with the highest standards of personal and professional integrity, not only on the company's premises but also at company-sponsored business, social events and elsewhere.

They shall be free from fraud and deception.

They shall always conform to the best standards of ethical conduct.

Corporate opportunities

All have a duty to the company to advance its legitimate interests when the opportunity arises.

FIGURE 11.2
CODE OF ETHICS AND BUSINESS CONDUCT, BIOCON INDIA (cont.)

Directors, officers and employees are expressly prohibited from:

☐ taking for themselves personally opportunities that are discovered through the use of the company's property, information or position;

☐ competing directly with the current business of the company or its likely future business;

☐ using company property, information, or position for personal gain.

If the company has made a final decision not to pursue an opportunity, an individual may follow it up only after disclosing the same to the board of directors or to the nominated committee or individual.

Confidentiality

All shall respect confidential information on the company, any of its customers, suppliers or business associates. Disclosure of such information should only be made where authorised or required by law.

The use of any confidential information for personal gain is strictly forbidden.

Fair dealing

All Biocon employees at all levels should deal fairly with those we do business with. No-one should take unfair advantage of anyone through manipulation, concealment, abuse of confidential information, misrepresentation of facts or any other unfair dealing practices.

Employees

The company will not tolerate discrimination on any grounds whatsoever. All employees will be treated fairly and given the opportunity to grow and develop within the company. Promotion will be on merit.

Bullying or harassment is regarded as a serious offence and will not be tolerated.

Protection and proper use of company assets

Everyone has a duty to protect the company's assets and ensure their proper use. Theft, carelessness and waste of company assets damage profitability. These assets should only be used for legitimate business purposes.

Compliance with laws, rules and regulations

All employed by the company shall comply with all relevant laws, rules and regulations. All employees at all levels are expected to know how these laws and rules apply to their area of decision-making. In the event of any uncertainty, the employee concerned should consult the company legal department before taking action.

Compliance with the code

If any person suspects or knows of a violation of this code, they must immediately report the same to the board of directors or the designated person or committee. The company has a whistle-blowing policy that will protect their anonymity; details of this are on the intranet.

Violations of this code will result in disciplinary action and, in some cases, dismissal. Full details of the disciplinary procedures and the appeal processes are included on the company intranet.

Interpretation of this code

Interpretation of this code is reserved for the board.

The board may appoint a designated committee or designated person to act on its behalf in interpreting and clarifying this code.

Honesty and integrity

Chapter 6 on effective leadership emphasised the importance of integrity for directors. Without this quality, a person is unlikely to be sufficiently interested in or guided by an ethical code.

The director who has integrity will want the organisation's values to be compatible with their own. They won't want to work for or lead an organisation they feel uncomfortable with.

Standards of acceptable behaviour are both objective and subjective. While there are some moral absolutes in business, some things that are clearly wrong (stealing, cheating, misappropriation of money, making false or deliberately misleading statements to the stock market, exploitation of workers etc.) there are grey areas, too. When do tactics to beat the competition become dirty tricks? When does "tough negotiation" become bullying or abuse of economic power? When do PR and "spin" become deception and lies? The individual will decide where the boundaries are according to their *personal ethical code*.

If the others in the organisation continually act outside these boundaries (with the blessing of the board), then the director with integrity has no choice but to leave.

Fiduciary duties

Central to business ethics is the concept of **fiduciary duty**. The director acts on behalf of others – the many people who trust them to act honestly, capably and in the **best interests of the organisation as a whole**. The company's assets are held for the benefit of others; they do not *belong* to the director. This is the legal principle that put newspaper tycoon Conrad Black in the dock.

The interests of the company must come before narrow self-interest.

Directors must absent themselves from discussions and decisions on subjects in which they have a personal financial interest. This applies even in cases where the interest is limited or indirect or lies with a family member.

Any real or potential conflict of interest must be disclosed to the board. Chapter 7 of *The Director's Handbook* discusses the circumstances in which a director may be in breach of their fiduciary duty in detail, but "when in doubt disclose" is a good dictum.

The director's position as a fiduciary means it's unethical for them to use "inside" information for direct or indirect personal gain. They must not trade their shares during "closed periods" – i.e. times when information likely to influence the movement of the company's share price has not been made available to the investing public. Trading will be blocked between balance dates and the announcement of results and when market-sensitive information – such as news of a takeover bid or new contract – has not been released. Again, chapter 7 of the *Handbook* includes much useful information on this.

Behaviours and culture

The IBE has identified five factors critical for an ethical culture.

☐ Leaders support and "model" ethical behaviour; they lead by example.

☐ Consistent communications come from leaders.

☐ Ethics are integrated into the organisation's goals, business processes and strategies.

☐ Ethics are part of the performance management system.

☐ Ethics are part of the recruitment process and selection criteria.

This reinforces the key points that the code must be followed and practised at the highest levels of the organisation and clearly communicated to every employee.

Assurance

The boards of some larger companies have an ethics committee, made up of non-executives. Its primary purpose is to monitor the non-financial aspects of management activity – ethical conduct, social and environmental responsibility, health and safety etc.

An ethics committee may be an imperative for high-risk sectors such as pharmaceuticals and oil and gas extraction and where a company trades with countries that are economically and politically "immature" and have different "ethical norms". For most others, it's probably unnecessary.

A separate committee on ethics may:

☐ divert the issue from the main board;

☐ duplicate the work of the audit and risk committee;

☐ "layer on" more process.

The main board should instead be able to provide assurance through an ethical health check. This can be carried out annually, or as the need arises. (An ad hoc review may be necessary when breaches of the ethical code are suspected.) Figure 11.3 on the next page is a list of questions for a "model" health check.

FIGURE 11.3
ETHICAL HEALTH CHECK FOR DIRECTORS

☐ Is there a clear policy, approved and reviewed annually by the board?

☐ Has the board considered, understood and agreed the process by which its values are embedded in the business?

☐ Is the policy set out in clear terms, communicated well throughout the organisation and agreed to as a part of individual employment contracts?

☐ Do staff members see adherence to the policy as an important part of their employment or more as "window dressing" for the company?

☐ Is the policy considered in appraisals and training and development?

☐ Is there an effective whistle-blowing policy and a procedure that protects the whistle-blower?

☐ Do ethical values inform the board's decision-making and choice of strategic initiatives?

☐ Does the board have mechanisms that measure ethics pragmatically?

Monitoring systems

How do you measure the ethical performance of the business? How do you judge the extent to which you've succeeded in embedding ethical values? Absence of law suits does not prove that's all as it should be.

There are several possible approaches to objective monitoring.

☐ An ethical survey, involving employees, suppliers and investors, can test the level of awareness of the code and the whistle-blowing policy. More than this, it can test the level of *confidence* in the code and the directors. Stakeholders will tell you whether the code is clear, concise and practised, and whether they'd fear the consequences of reporting a breach.

☐ Recording the number and nature of complaints, the number and nature of calls to the "ethical hotline", for example, will be a useful indication of the level of compliance. (Year-on-year comparisons of these records should, though, be used with caution. Decreases are not necessarily evidence of an improvement in performance; it may be that whistle-blowers have been reluctant to come forward/been frightened off.)

☐   Asking the internal audit function to report specifically on ethics in the business is a sensible option for larger companies. It will provide assurance (or not) that the building blocks exist across the organisation (particularly important, perhaps, where the geographical spread is wide), that the ethical code is understood and that decisions are compatible with it.

Ethical reporting

Looking through a selection of annual reports and accounts recently published in the UK, it's clear that the quality of ethical reporting is quite variable. Many policies are discussed in very general terms and are unsupported by metrics.

The most frequently mentioned topics are:

☐   responsibility to and participation in the communities in which the company operates;

☐   public health issues (particularly in the food and drink and pharmaceuticals sectors);

☐   fair employment practices and non-discrimination;

☐   environmental policy statements; plans to become a low-carbon company;

☐   health and safety issues;

☐   good citizenship – e.g. good pay and conditions in developing countries.

Convincing readers (investors, stakeholders, campaigning groups, the public etc.) that these issues are taken seriously depends on a more rigorous approach to reporting.

If people are to believe values and codes of conducts are more than well-meaning fluff they'll need facts and figures.

The good news is that an increasing number of companies now recognise this. There is a significant trend towards environmental reporting that includes performance metrics. This is seen especially in sectors exposed to high environmental risks – e.g. the oil and gas, chemicals or extractive industries – where some companies commission independent environmental audits and include the report in the annual report and accounts. However, retailers and makers of consumer goods are also starting to include more meaningful information.

Figure 11.4 lists information given by the UK based brewer and brand owner Scottish & Newcastle in its 2006 annual report.

FIGURE 11.4
SCOTTISH & NEWCASTLE PLC 2006 ANNUAL REPORT: NON-FINANCIAL MEASURES

Measures	Comment
Total water used by production volume (hl/hl) 2006 – 4.1 2005 – 4.5	**Our world** Scottish & Newcastle is a leading brewer in many parts of the world. We constantly seek to drive value in our mature markets and establish strong platforms in exciting emerging markets
Total energy used by production volume (kwh/hl) 2006 – 32.7 2005 – 37.6	**Our planet** We strive to reduce our impact on the environment by reducing our carbon footprint, investing in sustainable resources and encouraging recycling at all our production sites
Total CO_2 emissions by production volume kg CO_2/hl 2006 – 8.5 2005 – 9.5	**Our consumers** We seek to build our consumer base by innovating, building exciting brands and producing high-quality products
Serious injury rate per 1,000 employees 2006 – 22.9 2005 – 37.2	**Our values** We acknowledge our responsibilities as an alcohol producer, and seek to promote responsible drinking in all our worldwide markets. We seek to support our customers and suppliers in developing sustainable businesses
% of waste recycled 2006 – 94% 2005 – 93%	**Our people** We seek to develop our people and help them to rise to their full potential, to work in partnership with stakeholders both inside and outside the company, and to grow the business for the benefit of our communities and our shareholders

Ethics and the supply chain

A company must take reasonable care to ensure that its standards and ethical values are understood and adhered to by all its suppliers.

Furore followed War on Want revelations in December 2006 that Tesco, Primark and Asda, all members of the Ethical Trading Initiative, were using clothing factories in Bangladesh that paid less than the living wage and breached health and safety standards.

A requirement for ethics must be written into contracts with suppliers and business partners and it must be enforced. Mining company Rio Tinto has declared it's prepared to withdraw from business relationships if any partners do not live up to its values.

Marks and Spencer asks suppliers to sign up to minimum standards and makes clear that failure to ensure they're observed can lead to loss of contract.

Microsoft announced at the end of March 2007 that it had dropped one of its suppliers in the UK because it failed to meet the company's standards on employee diversity. Dave Gartenberg, the UK director of human resources, was quoted as saying, "Microsoft is committed to ensuring we have a diverse and inclusive workforce, and we want to work with companies that share these principles. Consequently, we are looking at how we can take a leadership position in driving positive change, while respecting local legislation".

This is a strong message to give to other companies.

Compliance with ethical codes and standards can be measured by a system of self-assessment (where the supplier reviews procedures and pay and conditions) and by spot checks and audits by the client/outsourcing company.

Summary

Ethical codes set the moral standards for directors (or, in the case of a charity, trustees) and all those working with and for them, including suppliers and their employees.

They mean nothing, however, without ethical behaviour. And that starts at the top. The board must act with integrity, with honesty and for the greater good of the company, its shareholders and stakeholders. Its members must not misuse the assets of the company or abuse their power.

To provide effective leadership on ethics, directors must have a close personal affinity with corporate values and principles. Where there are significant conflicts, where codes diverge, a director must leave the organisation.

The demand for "ethical intelligence" among business leaders – awareness of their wider responsibilities and an understanding of fair play – is probably at an all-time high. Ethics, like good governance, will build trust and confidence among shareholders, the public and stakeholders. They will strengthen an organisation's most valuable asset – its good name.

Ethics are good business.

APPENDIX
CURRENT BUSINESS ETHICS ISSUES

- ☐ Bullying and harassment

- ☐ Racial discrimination

- ☐ Corruption *(in the widest sense of misuse of entrusted power)*

- ☐ Conflicts of interest

- ☐ Dishonesty and fraud

- ☐ Diversity in the workplace

- ☐ Environmental impact

- ☐ Executive pay

- ☐ Human rights standards, including labour rights

- ☐ Marketing *(Is the company making false claims? Is it targeting vulnerable groups?)*

- ☐ Money laundering

- ☐ Payment terms for smaller firms

- ☐ Whistle-blowing arrangements

- ☐ The supply chain *(Do offshore centres meet the standards of the International Labour Organisation?)*

- ☐ Tax avoidance *(Are companies overly aggressive in exploiting "loopholes"? Are they putting back what they should?)*

- ☐ Work-life balance

Source: Living up to our Values, Institute of Business Ethics, 2006

bringing it all together

CHAPTER 12

Introduction

This chapter has two principal aims: to summarise the themes, ideas and purposes of the book in one "place"; to guide readers to the areas most relevant for them.

Using this book

Good business books stimulate thought, discussion and a re-evaluation of personal views. They require readers to think about what the author's saying and to decide where it would add value to their work.

One of my aims in writing this book has been to follow this tradition. I've not wanted to "hand out absolute truths" in the manner of Moses and the tablets of stone. I've wanted to *offer approaches* that are rooted in good theory and have been found to work well in practice; I've wanted to offer templates to draw from.

Read this book in the context of your own organisation.

The reach of this book

The Effective Director is written for a broad constituency. Both experienced directors and those preparing for the role will find it useful — whether they're in the public, private or not-for-profit sectors, whether they work for large or small organisations.

The book complements the IoD's Chartered Director development programme but it is not for Chartered Director candidates exclusively.

Although its legal frame of reference is UK law, the book crosses national boundaries. Its central themes – good corporate governance and best practice – are important for organisations all over the world.

The scope of this book

The role of director requires good working knowledge of relevant rules, regulations and codes. The individual must be clear about their legal responsibilities and potential liabilities and their fiduciary duties. They must know "the facts". **But this is the base position. The effective director has knowledge and experience far beyond this.**

Therefore, topics such as vision, mission and values, building personal effectiveness, leadership and the management of people are discussed in detail.

The book is packed with practical tools for better performance such as checklists, tables and case studies. But it's also a guide to good theory.

The synopsis

Chapter 1 on the role of the board examines the key elements of boardroom governance. It includes lots of practical examples; and it's up to the reader to assess how workable these are in their own environments.

The starting point is to agree those matters that only the board should decide. This achieves clarity – both for the board and those below board level. Figure 1.2 is a sample statement of reserved matters.

Attention is also drawn to the importance of having the right information, at the right time, so that directors get a clear and true picture of the health of the organisation.

The other key process is the board effectiveness review. This is an obvious tool for improving the performance of the board. It should be thorough but not complex. If the exercise is protracted and too heavy on "process", some of its value will be lost. Figure 1.4 shows what a typical review may cover.

The chapter makes clear that the relationship between chairman and chief executive is critical.

The case study on Cosgrove Manufacturing shows what can happen when the appointment of a new chief executive fails and board processes are inadequate.

Chapter 2 on duties and liabilities explains some of the key legal principles governing companies and those leading them. It also looks at the pivotal relationships with shareholders (including private equity investors) and stakeholders.

Figure 2.1 is a practical summary of the seven duties of directors set out in sections 171-177 of the Companies Act 2006.

The chapter also sets out the position of directors when the business is in financial difficulties.

It is vital that directors understand their obligations, responsibilities and potential liabilities. But these should not be allowed to cast a shadow over their role. There is no expectation in the law of infallibility: the basic requirement is for the director to act responsibly, honestly and with reasonable care.

The key message of this chapter is that the role of director is not a burden: it is an opportunity. Do it well and you will make an invaluable contribution to an organisation and achieve your personal best.

The central idea of **chapter 3** is that **governance** is an opportunity to add value. Get it right and you will improve the organisation's reputation among shareholders and stakeholders. You will increase shareholder value, for companies with good governance standards have higher market ratings.

The key is to see good governance as something other than a compliance-driven activity. It's not about ticking boxes to demonstrate political correctness: it's about observing those elements of best practice that make decision-making more robust and give directors more effective *control*.

The theme of good governance runs throughout the book, so this is the core chapter for all readers.

It will, however, be of special relevance to private companies considering flotation on the Stock Exchange, and ensure that appropriate value is obtained on listing. Commitment to the standards of good governance, laid down in the Combined Code, will give assurance to advisers and to investors.

The case study on Holden Services shows what a successful private company may have to do to get ready for flotation.

Organisations with good standards of governance will fulfil their purpose (their "mission") and live up to their values.

Chapter 4 focuses on the chairman and non-executive directors. It sets down their formal duties and the structures under which they operate, but it goes further than this, looking at the specific ways they can add value.

The bread and butter of the chairman's role may be the smooth and effective running of the meetings, but their impact extends beyond this.

Clear descriptions of the roles and tasks of chairman and chief executive will greatly assist their working relationship – as will a clear understanding of the kinds of issues that will normally be discussed between them.

Regular contact is essential. Some chairmen and chief executives meet weekly; others less frequently.

In my various roles as chairman, I've preferred to meet formally each month and have ad hoc meetings as necessary. The chief executive has been free to contact me at any time, day or night, if they need to.

Trust between chairman and chief executive is essential.

Non-executive directors are a valuable asset for any organisation – provided they've been carefully chosen and encouraged to learn about the organisation and contribute fully to the board.

The board effectiveness review and individual appraisals will improve their performance year by year.

The key committees of the board and their terms of reference are discussed in **chapter 5**.

The **remuneration committee** faces a delicate balancing act. Rewards for top executives must reflect their performance and they must be aligned with the interests of shareholders. At the same time, though, they must be sufficient to recruit, retain and motivate top talent.

The remuneration report will be examined closely by institutional investors and other shareholder groups. Clear explanation of the policy is essential.

The **nomination committee** meets much less frequently than the remco, but has the important role of managing the selection of directors. My preference is to see this committee led by the chairman of the company.

The **audit committee** plays a vital role in maintaining good controls and in supporting the board's determination to make governance add value. Its role, and ways to improve its performance, are therefore examined in detail.

The foundation for the audit committee is the risk assessment and control process, and this is discussed in a practical way towards the end of the chapter.

In this imperfect, fast-changing world, the demands on boards are great. All directors and those who aspire to the role will want to know how to improve their **personal effectiveness**.

Chapter 6 identifies the building blocks for better performance.

Winning trust is essential. This will not be achieved without integrity. Effective directors have an ethical code and live by it; their actions are consistent with their words.

Directors should be aware of the specific areas where they need to improve. The self-awareness checklist at Figure 6.1 will help them identify these.

They will also need to reflect on the general qualities for directors. Figure 6.6 lists the essential attributes.

Finally, they will need to understand how to deal with stress. Without this ability, they will lack the emotional resilience for consistent performance.

Stress, and ways to deal with it, are discussed in the last few sections.

Leadership is the topic of **chapter 7**. This chapter is short on definitions but long on practical observations about what makes leadership work.

The five dimensions of leadership given in Figure 7.1 are a good starting framework.

A great leader is very aware of their followers and their goals and aspirations. The 10 words most used by followers when describing a good leader are a useful insight. Think of these words and the behavioural characteristics and attributes given in figures 7.2 and 7.3 when thinking about your own leadership.

In recognition of the particular challenges they face and the adjustments they have to make, new directors are given a special section at the end of this chapter.

Chapter 8 explains how to get the most from the talent in the organisation.

The best organisations have:

☐ the right strategy and the right plan of implementation;

☐ the right people in the right places.

And they make sure that they marry the two. There must be close alignment between the vision, mission and values of the organisation and personal objectives and milestones for individuals. This is why appraisals are so important a part of effective people management.

People must be motivated and empowered to make decisions at the closest possible point of impact.

The board needs to make management development and succession planning an annual exercise. Potential future leaders need to be identified early and given the opportunity to develop on an accelerated path. The model of executive potential illustrated in Figure 8.2 is a useful analytical tool to summarise the talent in an organisation.

Small and medium-sized and family companies are the focus of **chapter 9**. For many of these, the challenge is how to observe best practice without layering on costly and unnecessary processes.

To help, I look at the minimum requirements for good governance, providing, at Figure 9.1, a governance checklist for SMEs.

Smaller companies can be vulnerable when they start to grow; standards of governance will need to keep pace.

The case study on McTavish Ltd spells out some of the issues facing family companies that need new sources of capital and new skills to support growth.

Owner-managers should remember the importance of good, independent advice. A non-executive director, a mentor, or a trusted adviser can make a big difference.

Chapter 10 is another special-topic chapter, dealing with charities and not-for-profit organisations.

Again, the approach is to guide directors and trustees towards the issues they need to be thinking about. Figure 10.1 sets out the high-level areas of focus, but it is not a "prescription". It is more of a suggestion, a starting point, drawn from best practice.

Figure 10.5 sets out a template for evaluating an NPO – a health check for trustees.

The key message is that running a successful charity or an NPO has much in common with running a successful commercial enterprise. This is underlined by the case study on Mid Yorkshire Hospitals Trust. Kindly provided by the trust's chairman, Sir Hugh Sykes, this shows the value private-sector principles can bring to public-sector organisations.

Last but by no means least, is the discussion on **ethics** in **chapter 11**.

The case for business ethics is not only moral but also pragmatic. Ethics build reputations; and reputations are assets.

The ethical code of an organisation and the ethical codes of its directors must converge. Where there are material conflicts, organisations and boards fail each other.

There needs, too, to be the utmost consistency between ethics and behaviour. An ethical code will, like a statement of values, be meaningless unless followed in practice.

Consistency is achieved by:

- leading by example;
- communicating clearly with employees;
- making ethics part of the management performance system;
- making ethics a factor in recruitment and the choice of suppliers.

CODA

- The effective director has knowledge and skills but understands that the state of perfection is never reached, that professional development is continuous.
- The effective director is curious, searching out new and better ways of doing things.
- The effective director is focussed on those things that add greater value, and is an excellent implementer of practical initiatives that are aligned with their organisation's strategy.
- The effective director understands the difference between risk-taking and recklessness, and is able to optimise the risk-reward trade-off.
- The effective director has the courage to stand up for what they believe in and the humility to invite and accept constructive challenge.
- The effective director thinks about their legacy and understands the importance of succession planning.
- The effective director says "people are our greatest asset" and proves they mean it.
- The effective director is conscientious but understands the need for work-life balance.

summary of the Combined Code on Corporate Governance and the Turnbull Guidance

APPENDIX I

1. Introduction

The Combined Code on Corporate Governance incorporates recommendations made by committees led by Sir Adrian Cadbury (1992), Sir Richard Greenbury (1995), Sir Ronnie Hampel (1998), Sir Derek Higgs and Sir Robert Smith (2003) and the Turnbull Guidance, published in 1999 and updated in 2005. It was last revised in June 2006.

The Combined Code applies to companies listed on the London Stock Exchange on a "comply or explain" basis, that is, listed companies are expected to comply with the Code's provisions most of the time and to give a considered explanation to shareholders of any departures from its provisions.

In practice, the Combined Code and the Turnbull Guidance have relevance to nearly all companies and organisations. The following extracts should be of interest to directors of most companies and organisations, irrespective of size and whether or not the company is quoted.

2. The Combined Code

Board of Directors

The board

☐ Every company should be headed by an effective board, which is collectively responsible for the success of the company.

☐ The board's role is to provide entrepreneurial leadership of the company within a framework of prudent controls which enables risk to be assessed and managed.

☐ The board should set the company's strategic aims, ensure the necessary financial and human resources are in place for the company to meet its objectives and review management performance.

☐ The board should set the company's values and standards and ensure that its obligations to its shareholders and others are understood and met.

☐ All directors must take decisions objectively in the interests of the company.

☐ As part of their role as members of the board, non-executive directors should constructively challenge and help develop proposals on strategy.

☐ The board should meet sufficiently regularly to discharge its duties effectively.

☐ There should be a formal schedule of matters reserved for its decision.

Chairman and chief executive

- ☐ There should be a clear division of responsibilities at the head of the company between the running of the board and the executive responsibility for the running of the company's business.

- ☐ No one individual should have unfettered powers of decision.

- ☐ The roles of chairman and chief executive should not be exercised by the same individual and the division of responsibilities between the chairman and the chief executive should be clearly established, set out in writing and agreed by the board.

- ☐ The chairman is responsible for leadership of the board on all aspects of its role and setting its agenda.

- ☐ The chairman is also responsible for ensuring that the directors receive accurate, timely and clear information.

- ☐ The chairman should ensure effective communication with shareholders.

- ☐ The chairman should also facilitate the effective contribution of non-executive directors in particular and ensure constructive relations between executive and non-executive directors.

Board balance and independence

- ☐ The board should include a balance of executive and non-executive directors (and in particular independent non-executive directors, as defined by the Code – see Code Provision A.3.1) such that no individual or small group of individuals can dominate the board's decision taking.

- ☐ The board should not be so large as to be unwieldy. The board should be of sufficient size that the balance of skills and experience is appropriate for the requirements of the business and that changes to the board's composition can be managed without undue disruption.

Information and professional development

- ☐ The board should be supplied in a timely manner with information in a form and of a quality appropriate to enable it to discharge its duties. Management has an obligation to provide such information but directors should seek clarification or amplification where necessary.

- ☐ All directors should receive induction on joining the board and should regularly update and refresh their skills and knowledge.

- ☐ The board should ensure that all directors have access to independent professional advice at the company's expense where they judge it necessary to discharge their responsibilities as directors.

Performance evaluation

- [ ] The board should undertake a formal and rigorous annual evaluation of its own performance, that of its committees and individual directors.
- [ ] Individual evaluation should aim to show whether each director continues to contribute effectively and to demonstrate commitment to the role.
- [ ] The chairman should act on the results of the performance evaluation.

Re-election

- [ ] All directors should be submitted for re-election at regular intervals, subject to continued satisfactory performance.
- [ ] The board should ensure planned and progressive refreshing of the board.
- [ ] Non-executive directors should be appointed for specific terms and any term beyond six years should be subject to a particularly rigorous review.

Board committees

- [ ] The Combined Code contains recommendations for the composition and terms of reference for audit, remuneration and nomination committees.

Remuneration

- [ ] Levels of remuneration should be sufficient to attract, retain and motivate directors of the quality required to run the company successfully, but a company should avoid paying more than is necessary for this purpose.
- [ ] A significant proportion of executive directors' remuneration should be structured so as to link rewards to corporate and individual performance. Schedule A in the Combined Code contains provisions on the design of performance-related remuneration.
- [ ] There should be a formal and transparent procedure for developing policy on executive remuneration and for fixing the remuneration of individual directors.
- [ ] No director should be involved in deciding his or her own remuneration.

Relations with Shareholders

- [ ] There should be a dialogue with shareholders based on the mutual understanding of objectives. The board as a whole has the responsibility for ensuring that a satisfactory dialogue with shareholders takes place.
- [ ] The board should use the AGM to communicate with investors and to encourage their participation.

Accountability and Audit

Financial reporting

The board should present a balanced and understandable assessment of the company's position and prospects by ensuring that:

☐ both directors and auditors explain their reporting responsibilities in financial reports;

☐ financial reports are on a "going concern" basis, including an explanation of assumptions and qualifications.

Internal Control

The board should maintain a sound system of internal control to safeguard the shareholders' investment and the company's assets by:

☐ conducting an annual review of such controls; and

☐ reviewing the need for an internal audit function on a regular basis, where the company does not have one.

Auditors

☐ The board should establish formal and transparent arrangements for considering how they should apply the financial reporting and internal control principles and for maintaining an appropriate relationship with the company's auditors.

3. The Turnbull Guidance

Approach

☐ The Turnbull Guidance provides guidance on how the board can maintain a sound system of internal control to safeguard shareholders' investment and the company's assets and how the board should review the effectiveness of the company's system of internal control.

☐ Internal control includes financial, operational and compliance controls and risk management.

☐ The purpose of internal control is to help manage and control risk appropriately, rather than to eliminate all risks, since profits are in part the reward for successful risk-taking in business.

☐ The board should adopt a risk-based approach to establishing a sound system of internal control, involving an assessment of risks faced by the company, determining what control activities are required to avoid or reduce the impact of those risks and ensuring that appropriate and timely information is communicated to directors to enable them to monitor performance and respond rapidly where change is required.

☐ The risks to be managed should depend on the business, but should encompass more than just financial risk.

☐ The board should regularly receive and review reports on internal control and undertake an annual assessment.

☐ The adoption of a risk-based internal control system should be embedded in the company's business processes, linked to the business objectives and not be just a separate exercise undertaken to meet regulatory requirements. In order to ensure that the system is not just left to run on its own, managers are required to report on specific areas assigned to them.

☐ Procedures and the frequency of reporting required should be communicated and agreed so that major control weaknesses may be reported immediately.

Board Responsibilities

☐ The board must set appropriate policies on internal control, seek regular assurance that the system is working satisfactorily, and ensure that the system is effective in managing risks.

☐ In setting its policy, the board should consider the following factors.

 ☐ *The nature and extent of the risks facing company, which risks are acceptable and to what extent.*

 ☐ *The likelihood of the risks materialising.*

 ☐ *The company's ability to reduce the incidence and impact on the business of risks that do materialise.*

 ☐ *The cost of operating particular controls relative to the benefits of managing the associated risks.*

☐ The board is responsible for reviewing the effectiveness of the internal control system. The Appendix to the Guidance sets out key questions that a board may wish to consider when assessing the effectiveness of the company's internal control system.

Chartered Director Code of Professional Conduct

APPENDIX II

This Code has been written in order to help directors meet high standards of professionalism and ethics. The Code provides guidance to directors and lays down the standards that the Institute expects of Chartered Directors.

The purpose of the Code

One of the IoD's fundamental aims is to increase the professionalism of its members. To further this aim, it requires all Chartered Directors to adhere to the Code of Professional Conduct, as a way of providing tangible evidence of their commitment to professionalism and probity. Chartered Directors who breach the Code may be subject to disciplinary action by the Institute.

Chartered Directors represent a wide range of sectors and organisations. This reflects the desire of public, charitable, private and other organisations to adopt good governance and practice. The term "company", which is used throughout the Code, is not meant to exclude public-sector bodies, charities and NPOs.

The Code of Professional Conduct

(All references to the masculine gender include the feminine)

A Chartered Director ("director") shall:

Article 1

Exercise leadership, enterprise and judgement in directing the company so as to achieve its continuing prosperity and act in the best interests of the company as a whole.

A director should recognise that, as a member of the board, he has individual and collective responsibility for enterprise and the exercise of commercial judgement in his company. Each director should endeavour to ensure that the board fulfils its key purpose of safeguarding and improving the company's prosperity.

A director should endeavour to make certain that the responsibilities of the board have been specified clearly and are properly understood. A director should be diligent in discharging his duties to the company and must acquire a broad knowledge about the business of the company and the statutory and regulatory requirements affecting company direction.

A director should aim to attend all board meetings.

Article 2

Follow the standards of good practice set out in the Institute's publications* and act accordingly and diligently.

A director should endeavour to ensure that the board is properly constituted and managed, addresses its key tasks and devotes sufficient time to address each of them properly.

A director should always assist his board in ensuring that the board establishes vision, mission and values for the company, sets strategy, delegates appropriately to management, is accountable to shareholders and holds itself responsible to relevant stakeholders.

A director should insist that the board is provided with sufficient regular and timely information to enable the directors to discharge their duties of care and diligence. If adequate or timely information is not provided, the director should make an appropriate objection. Any objection, and the reasons for it, should be included in board minutes. An internal audit of systems supporting the board should be conducted regularly.

A director should endeavour to make sure that access between the board and the auditors is open and unimpeded. A director should be satisfied that the scope of the audit is adequate and that management and any internal auditors have co-operated fully.

Article 3

Serve the legitimate interests of the company's shareholders.

A director should endeavour to ensure, acting as a member of the board, that the company is financially viable, and properly managed so as to protect and enhance the interests of the company and its shareholders over time.

A director should seek to understand the expectations of shareholders and endeavour to fulfil them when deciding upon the best interests of the company. A director should seek to ensure that proper communication is made with shareholders on the general strategies being adopted for the company and on other matters of importance, bearing in mind the needs of commercial security and Stock Exchange and other compliance requirements where appropriate.

**Standards for the Board* (2006), *The Director's Handbook* (2007) and *The Effective Director* (2008).

A director should seek to ensure that all shareholders or classes of shareholders are treated fairly according to their relative rights.

Article 4

Exercise responsibilities to employees, customers, suppliers and other relevant stakeholders, including the wider community.

Whilst the obligations of a director are primarily owed to the company, it is also necessary to take into account the interests of all individuals and groups which the board judges have a legitimate interest in the achievement of company objectives and the way in which these objectives are achieved.

A director should ensure that the board identifies and knows the interests, views and expectations of these stakeholders. He should ensure that communications with such parties are timely, effective and unbiased, subject to the needs of commercial security and regulatory compliance where appropriate.

A director should help his board to promote goodwill with stakeholders and be prepared to be accountable for company actions.

A director should encourage the board to set up procedures for managing relationships with stakeholders, particularly at times of crisis (eg litigation, environmental disasters, takeover bids).

Article 5

Comply with relevant laws, regulations and codes of practice, refrain from anti-competitive practices, and honour obligations and commitments.

A director must at all times comply with the law and should endeavour to ensure that his company at all times complies with the law governing its operations. In evaluating the interests of the company, a board of directors is accountable to the shareholders as a whole, but various Acts of Parliament have imposed wider responsibilities on companies and directors so that directors must evaluate their actions in a broader social context and must be conscious of the impact of their business on society. Particular attention should be paid to the environment, questions of occupational health and safety, employee relations, equal opportunity for employees, the impact of competition rules and consumer protection rules, and other legislative and regulatory initiatives that may arise from time to time.

A director of a company whose securities are listed on the Stock Exchange should ensure that the company complies with the listing rules. In particular he must observe those rules relating to any benefits that a director or an associated person may receive from the company by way of an issue of shares or any other transaction of a similar nature.

Article 6

At all times have a duty to respect the truth and act honestly in his business dealings and in the exercise of all his responsibilities as a director.

A director should not obtain, attempt to obtain, or accept, any bribe, secret commission or illegal inducement of any kind.

A director must be prepared, if necessary, to express disagreement with colleagues, including the chairman, chief executive or managing director.

A director should accept that resignation or dismissal may sometimes be the ultimate consequence of sustained protest on a matter of conscience or judgement.

However, if there is no need to express disagreement, a director should be prepared to accept collective responsibility and implement the decisions of the board as a loyal member of the board.

If a director is in doubt whether a proposed course of action is consistent with his fiduciary duties, then he should not support the course of action. Independent advice should be sought as soon as possible to clarify the issue.

When a director concludes that he is unable to acquiesce in a decision of the board, some or all of the following steps should be considered:

a   making his dissent and its possible consequences clear to the board as a means of seeking to influence the decision;

b   asking for additional legal, accounting or other professional advice;

c   asking that the decision be postponed to the next meeting to allow time for further consideration and informal discussion;

d   tabling a statement of dissent or writing to the chairman and asking that the statement or letter be minuted;

e   calling a special board meeting to consider the matter;

f   resigning and considering advising the appropriate regulator.

A director who chooses to resign on a point of principle should consider disclosing the reasons for resignation to shareholders or to the appropriate regulator, though a director should bear in mind the duty not to disclose confidential information.

Article 7

Avoid conflict between his personal interests, or the interests of any associated company or person, and his duties to the company.

A director must not take improper advantage of the position of director to gain, directly or indirectly, a personal advantage or an advantage for any associated person which might cause detriment to the company. A director should not use inside information for gain.

The personal interests of a director, and those of associated persons, must not take precedence over those of the company's shareholders generally.

A director should seek to avoid conflicts of interest wherever possible. Full and prior disclosure of any conflict, or potential conflict, must be made to the board. Where an actual or potential conflict does arise, a director should at least refrain from participating in the debate and/or voting on the matter, and in the extreme case of continuing material conflict of interest, should resign from the board. The board should develop guidelines on the circumstances in which benefits to be received by a director or an associated person are of sufficient magnitude that the approval of the shareholders should be sought, even if not required by law. The board should inform shareholders of these guidelines.

A director must not buy or sell shares while in possession of confidential information as a director of a company which, if disclosed publicly, would be likely to affect materially the price of the company's shares. The board should lay down precisely when shares can be traded by a director of a company, subject to legal or regulatory restrictions.

A director who is appointed to a board at the instigation of a party with a substantial interest in the company, such as a major shareholder or a creditor, should recognise the potential for a conflict of interest. The director's duty is to make a contribution in the interests of the company and the shareholders as a whole and not only in the interest of the interested party. Confidential matters should not be disclosed to such interested parties without the prior agreement of the board.

Where obligations to other people or bodies may preclude a director from taking an independent position on an issue, the director should disclose the position to the board, and it is for the board to judge whether or not he should take part in the board's consideration of the issue.

A director from time to time may need expert advice in order to discharge his duties properly. Separate independent advice should always be sought by a director on matters that may affect his position vis-à-vis the company.

Article 8

Not make improper use of information acquired as a director or disclose, or allow to be disclosed, information confidential to the company.

A director must not make improper use of information acquired by virtue of his position as a director. This prohibition applies irrespective of whether or not the director or any associated person would gain directly or indirectly a personal advantage or whether or not the company would be harmed.

A director must not disclose, or allow to be disclosed, confidential information received in the course of the exercise of his duties as a director, unless that disclosure has been authorised by the board of the company or is required by law. Matters such as trade secrets, processes, advertising and promotional programmes, and statistics affecting financial results are particularly sensitive and must not be disclosed.

A director should make sure that any information which is not publicly available and which would have a material effect on the company's share price is not provided to anyone who may be influenced to subscribe for, buy or sell shares, or may advise others to do so. Such information includes, but is not limited to: profit forecasts, proposed share issues, borrowings, impending take-overs, impending litigation, significant changes in operations, new products, new discoveries, and financial problems. Directors of a company listed on the Stock Exchange should ensure that adequate and timely disclosure is made to the Stock Exchange. In addition, they must not knowingly or recklessly disseminate false or misleading information to the market.

Article 9

Not recklessly or maliciously injure the professional reputation of another member of the Institute of Directors and not engage in any practice detrimental to the reputation and interests of the Institute or of the profession of director.

This Article covers all behaviour which unjustifiably brings the profession or the Institute into disrepute. It is impossible to list all instances where questions of duties to the profession of company direction and to colleagues may arise. However, there is a continuous and comprehensive duty on all members of the Institute to act in such a way as to uphold the dignity and reputation of the profession, and to conform with any specific requirements that the Institute may prescribe in connection with particular circumstances.

A director is obliged to uphold the traditions of the Institute and to strive to maintain and improve its reputation.

A director should always act with integrity towards the Institute; he should declare his position if faced with a conflict of interest when representing the Institute; and he should not knowingly misrepresent the views or policies of the Institute. He should not purport to represent the Institute without the express or implied authority of the Institute.

A director should respect the professional standing of other members of the Institute.

Ultimately, the conduct of companies depends upon the propriety and behaviour of those engaged in directing them. A director should therefore accept the responsibility to contribute personally to the efficiency and welfare of the profession as a part of the professional concept of service to the community.

Article 10

Keep abreast of current good practice.

A director should keep abreast of both practical and theoretical developments in direction to ensure that his expertise is constantly relevant. Directors should refer to the guidance issued by the Institute (which can be accessed on the website), to ascertain how this obligation may be put into practice. To access the online facility for updating CPD and to review the guidance, please log in to the website as usual. Once logged in, click on the "Access Chartered Director Online" link at the top of the welcome page. If you have any problems logging in or have any questions please email cdir.online@iod.com or telephone 020 7766 8951.

Continuous and rapid change is the norm in business and it is the responsibility of a director continually and systematically to add to his knowledge and expertise; it is not enough to match present good practice and thereafter regard oneself as adequately equipped for the future. CPD is mandatory for all Chartered Directors and must be submitted annually.

Article 11

Set high personal standards by keeping aware of and adhering to this Code, both in the spirit and in the letter, and promoting it to other directors.

A director must honour the Code in the spirit as well as in the letter. No Code can be all-embracing. It is not possible to identify every circumstance in which the provisions of this Code need to be applied and, undoubtedly, there are many circumstances not mentioned in the Code in which the conduct and integrity and enterprise of a director must be of considerable importance. The Code is not intended to prohibit only those kinds of conduct specified; or to allow things it does not expressly rule out.

When questions arise which are not covered explicitly by the Code, personal adherence to the generally accepted principles of honesty, professionalism and justice should determine a director's behaviour.

A director is expected to use common sense in applying the spirit of the Code, but the intention of the Code is that members should consistently meet a standard higher than basic acceptable requirements.

A director is expected to bring the same high standard of integrity to his non-business life as is demanded in his professional activities when these spheres of activity overlap.

A director must not knowingly cause or, where he has the power to prevent, permit any other party to be in breach of this Code or be a party to a breach.

Article 12

Apply the principles of this Code appropriately when acting as a director of a non-commercial organisation.

Many aspects of this Code apply specifically to commercial companies. However, many of the principles will be applicable to directors of other types of organisation.

If there is any doubt, directors of such organisations should always endeavour to apply the spirit of this Code and its general principles.

June 2007

glossary of terms

Audit committee A committee of the board made up of non-executive directors, at least one of whom must have recent and relevant financial experience. Their role is to review the accounts and to monitor the control environment.

Balanced scorecard A management reporting system that gives a view of the health of the business based on factors such as innovation and learning, customer satisfaction and internal business processes as well as financial performance.

Career development review The planning of steps in an individual's career.

Chairman A person of either sex who runs/leads the board and manages its business.

Chief executive A person who leads/runs the organisation.

Competencies Broadly based behavioural capabilities such as planning and organising, and making formal presentations.

Corporate governance The rules and procedures to ensure that a company or other organisation is properly run.

Culture The personality and character of the organisation derived over time and recognised by those who work in, or closely with, the organisation.

Inspirational leadership See transformational leadership, below.

IPO Initial public offering of shares.

Management letter A confidential letter sent by external auditors highlighting any weaknesses in a company's financial control environment.

Mission A statement of what needs to be done to achieve the organisation's vision (see below).

Nomination committee A committee of the board appointed to select new directors and the company secretary and, where necessary, remove existing directors.

Non-executive director A director who does not take part in the day-to-day activities of the operations of the company and who is appointed to the board for their wider knowledge and good judgment.

NPOs Not-for-profit organisations, including charities.

Perspirational leadership The practical aspects of leadership needed to deliver the vision and mission of an organisation – for example, strategic processes, aligned reward systems.

Private equity Funds provided by a venture capitalist for the "buy-out" of public companies or for the development and growth of small or family companies.

Remuneration committee A committee of the board made up of non-executive directors for setting top-level remuneration and incentive plans.

Risk assessment and control The identification of high-level risks and their subsequent management; a key process for the control environment and, indeed, for the evaluation of strategic alternatives.

Senior independent director The non-executive director designated to be a point of contact for shareholders who have concerns about the company and/or its board.

Stakeholders Individuals or groups whom the board judges have an interest in and/or influence over the company's operations and the achievement of its goals. They may include customers, employees, suppliers, distributors, joint venture partners, the local community, bankers and shareholders.

Strategy A statement of what the company will do, and the resources it will deploy, in order to fulfil its mission.

Succession planning Thinking about what will happen when key individuals leave. Includes long-term and emergency succession plans.

Three hundred and sixty degree evaluation Evaluation of an individual by themselves, their boss, their peers and their colleagues. (Also known as 360° feedback.)

Traits Relatively long-lasting and habitual characteristics of an individual.

Transformational leadership (Sometimes referred to as inspirational leadership.) A theory of leadership that emphasises the power of individuals to inspire followers to perform beyond their normal expectations by emphasising higher levels of need and fulfilment.

Values A set of principles, standards of conduct and deeply held beliefs that drive the decision-making of a company or other organisation.

Vision A view of the desired future state of the company or organisation used to inspire and motivate others

references

Bain, Neville, *Successful Management*, Macmillan, 1995

Bain, Neville, and David Band, *Winning Ways through Corporate Governance*, Macmillan, 1996

Bain, Neville, and Bill Mabey, *The People Advantage*, Macmillan, 2000

Beehr, Terry A, *Psychological Stress in the Workplace*, Routledge, 1995

Belbin, Meredith R, *Team Roles at Work*, Butterworth-Heinemann, 1997

Bennis, Warren, *On Becoming a Leader*, Hutchinson Business Books, 1990

Cadbury, Sir Adrian, *The Company Chairman*, Director Books, Simon and Schuster International Group, 1990

Carver, John, *Boards That Make a Difference*, Jossey-Bass, 1990

Charity Commission, *The Essential Trustee: What You Need to Know*, February 2007

Cliffe, Sarah, *Human Resources: Winning the War for Talent*, Harvard Business Review, September-October, 1998

Colley, John L, Jacqueline L Doyle, George W Logan and Wallace Stettinius, *Corporate Governance*, McGraw Hill, 2003

Covey, Stephen M R, and Rebecca R Merrill, *The Speed of Trust: The One Thing That Changes Everything*, Free Press, 2006

Dando, Nicole, and Walter Raven, *Living Up To Our Values: Developing Ethical Assurance*, Institute of Business Ethics, 2006

Department of Trade and Industry, *Number of Trade Unions and Membership in Great Britain, 1975-2002*

Ernst and Young, *Board Members on Risk: Leveraging Frameworks for the Future*, 2006

European Industrial Observatory, *Trade Union Membership 1993-2003*

Foster Back, Philippa, *Setting the Tone: Ethical Business Leadership*, Institute of Business Ethics, 2005

Gardner, Howard, and Emma Laskin, *Leading Minds: An Anatomy of Leadership*, Harper Collins Business, 1996

Goldsmith, Marshall, *What Got You Here Won't Get You There,* Hyperion, 2007

Goleman, Daniel, *Emotional Intelligence*, Bloomsbury, 1996

Grant, Gavin, chapter 4, *A Director's Guide to Corporate Governance*, Institute of Directors, 2004

Grant Thornton, *Corporate Governance Review 2006*, Grant Thornton, 2007

Handy, Charles, *The Hungry Spirit*, Hutchinson, 1997

Harrison, Debbie, *It's Time to Talk: The urgent need for dialogue to strengthen governance of UK pension schemes*, Economist Intelligence Unit, 2007

Huffington, Clare, *Stress at Work, Organisations and People*, Quarterly Journal of AMED, Kogan Page, August, 1997

Kouzes, James M, and Barry Z Posner, *The Leadership Challenge*, Jossey-Bass, 2002

Lipton, Phillip, *The demise of HIH: Corporate Governance Lessons, Keeping Good Companies*, Chartered Secretaries Australia, June, 2003

Lofthouse, Gareth, *CEO Briefing: Corporate Priorities for 2005*, Economist Intelligence Unit, 2005

Monks, Robert A G, and Nell Minnow, *Corporate Governance*, Blackwell Business, 1995

Neilson, Gary L, Bruce A Pasternack and Karen E Van Nuys, *The Passive-Aggressive Organisation*, Harvard Business Review, October, 2005

Neilson, Gary L, and Bruce A Pasternack, *The Cat That Came Back*, Booz Allen Hamilton, 2005

Odgers, Ian, *The Common Ingredients of Leadership, Board Paper Series*, Odgers Ray and Berndtson

Pascale, Richard T, *Managing on the Edge*, Simon and Schuster, 1990

Pfeffer, Jeffrey, *Competitive Advantage through People: Unleashing the Power of the Workforce*, Harvard Business Press, 1994

Pfeffer, Jeffrey, *The Human Equation: Building Profits by Putting People First*, Harvard Business Press, 1998

Prokesch, Steven E, *Unleashing the Power of Learning: An Interview with British Petroleum's John Browne*, Harvard Business Review, September-October, 1997

Starr, Randy, Jim Newfrock and Michael Delurey, *Enterprise Resilience: Managing Risk in the Networked Economy*, Booz Allen Hamilton, 2006

The Institute of Internal Auditors UK and Ireland, *Gaining Assurance on Risks*, 2006

Thomas, Chris, David Kidd and Claudio Fernandez-Aroaz, *Are You Underutilising Your Board?*, MIT Sloan Management Review, Winter, 2007

Webley, Simon, *Making Business Ethics Work: The Foundations of Effective Embedding*, Institute of Business Ethics, 2006

Willis, Michael and Michael Fass, *Faith in Governance: Renewing the Role of the Director*, Industrial Christian Fellowship, 2004

index